Board Dynamics

managing the battle in the boardroom

by

Tony Kellett

Grosvenor House
Publishing Limited

Cover design and graphics by Briony Donnachie.
For more of her work see www.brionydonnachie.com

The author can be contacted at
dynamics@boardroomassociates.co.uk

ISBN 978-1-907211-12-6

Acknowledgements

This book spun out of a conversation with a director at a large private equity company. He was concerned that he and his colleagues did not fully understand what drove the other directors on the boards of their investee companies and wanted to get a view from the 'other side' of the board table. Steve Soden and I developed some initial thoughts for a workshop. Steve produced some diagrams which form part of the text. The rest grew from there.

David Buckle has provided very useful guidance to shape the book more effectively. Margaret Dewhurst has made an invaluable contribution. Sally Butler has been particularly helpful in developing the chapter on communication. David Rose has provided further input. His insight and incisive comments have assisted greatly in delivering a finished product. Jean Grimley proof read the text assiduously and helped to refine the structure. Any errors that remain in the text or the content are mine and mine alone.

I must also thank the many people with whom I have sat on boards and those who have talked to me about their experiences on and with boards. Listening to and working with them has provided me with most of the background for this book.

Last but not least, I must thank my dear wife, Mary, who supported me through many years of working on boards and who has helped me through the process of getting this book from concept into print.

Preface

Board dynamics

Effective board performance is a key element in the success of any organisation. Every board has very significant responsibilities and yet the process of building and running the board typically takes little or no account of the way in which the members of the board interact with each other – the board dynamics. Good board dynamics can greatly improve the performance of the organisation. Bad board dynamics can severely damage the performance of organisations that are otherwise sound. The objective of the book is to give current and aspiring board members an insight into the nature of board behaviour and how board dynamics affect this.

Excellence should be the norm for boards, both in terms of the quality of the people sitting on them and their own effectiveness. The latter requires excellent communication to ensure that the strength of the individuals is harnessed to give broad yet incisive decision-making. Poor board dynamics impair board operation by undermining communication and hence decision-making.

The legal responsibilities of a board are largely independent of the size of the organisation that it governs but the approach of the board can be very different according to size. For example, directors of FTSE 250 companies are expected to add significant value and they often seek a lot of advice and support from outside the organisation to validate their decisions. The choice of potential directors and the pool of experience that is available to major organisations are both very large, making it easier for the board to be well-balanced.

In contrast, the boards of smaller companies, commonly called small and medium-sized enterprises (SMEs), have much greater financial constraints and may have limited choice of who sits on the board. Their directors may be too close to the day to day management of the business or they can become sounding boards for the major stakeholders. Therefore, smaller companies are more vulnerable to problems with board dynamics. However, when there are problems with large companies then the results can be much more serious.

Whilst such divergence reflects the more formal regulatory framework and visibility that the institutional investors in major companies expect, the accountability and personal responsibility of board members is determined by the same rules and laws and so the approach to board operation should not alter. There is a concern that smaller businesses can fail to recognise the added value that a board can bring. Effective board performance will be felt throughout the organisation and all board members must attempt to ensure that the board as a whole achieves this goal.

Every board has different characteristics which depend on the type of organisation, its maturity and the styles and experience of the individual members of the board. As an organisation and its market position develop, especially for early stage businesses, the requirements of the board can change considerably. Therefore, the board itself should be regarded as a dynamic entity that needs to evolve if it is to provide the best guidance for the organisation.

People who become directors frequently have particular backgrounds, for example with proven skills in management, marketing or innovation. They also usually have strong personalities. A mix of strong personalities can be a recipe for conflict unless the impact of these is fully understood and managed by the board, under the leadership of the chairman (throughout the book this term is meant to imply people of either sex, rather than use the less common term chairperson). The correct choice of board members is, therefore, a key element in determining the potential of the organisation. It is important that the organisation is wary of confusing the expert role with that of the professional leader and board member, particularly in specialist areas such as technology companies.

Nationality and culture play a very important role in board dynamics because the scope for misinterpretation increases significantly. Different cultural backgrounds have a huge impact on the interaction between board members. This is particularly important on the boards of multi-national organisations where it is essential to understand the cultural influences both across the organisation and within the board itself but many SMEs also operate internationally and have culturally diverse boards. The legal environment also varies considerably between countries, placing different burdens and responsibilities on board members. An experienced board member from another country may have a different approach to board responsibilities and behaviour. Whilst this can add tremendous value to a board, it needs to be understood and managed carefully.

Corporate governance focuses on the mechanics and processes of board operation. Various techniques have been developed to assess formal board performance, some being based on the British Financial Reporting Council's *Combined Code on Corporate Governance* which looks at the procedural dimension of a board. A review of board dynamics provides a totally separate dimension and is an important input to help a board monitor and improve its performance. Using these two components in conjunction can add significantly to understanding the underlying reasons behind the way a board performs.

Following the collapse of Enron in 2001 and Marconi in 2005 for example, the increased pressures on boards make it essential that this critical element of personal interaction on the board is fully understood. Such issues form part of a broader scope of corporate governance that each board should review. They are already regarded as a key factor for some investors in maximising their return on investment.

The burden of responsibility for delivering shareholder value falls on the directors themselves. It is extremely difficult for a member of the board to be truly objective about the performance of the board and his or her individual impact on it. This is particularly important, both for executives and for directors who represent major shareholders or whose responsibilities and loyalties extend to a broader set of stakeholders. This means that the responsibility for monitoring board dynamics issues has to be spread across the board with the chairman taking the lead.

Every organisation has critical issues. Some are current; some are latent. It is the role of the board to identify and resolve these issues without delay. A frequently overlooked question that directors should ask themselves is 'how much of the issue am I?'

The structure of the book

This book is a practitioner's guide and is based on hard, pragmatic experience of working on boards. It provides insights into the issues that drive board dynamics and raises questions that need to be answered in order to deliver a sustainable, high quality performance by the board. Its objective is to provide information and stimulus to develop and maintain effective board operation. It is targeted at those who recruit and manage boards, at current and aspiring directors and at those who interact with board members. It offers a model for looking at board roles and how they impact on the effectiveness of the board as a whole. In particular, it emphasises the view that board dynamics can make the difference between 'the whole being greater than the sum of the parts' and the 'chain is as strong as its weakest link' models of group effectiveness.

It does not set out to tell seasoned directors anything that they should not already be implicitly aware of but, by putting together all the information in one place and making the ideas explicit, it aims to provide a powerful overview, insight and a useful repository.

Organisations vary considerably, both in terms of their function and their stage of development. The nature of the board needs to reflect the needs of the organisation and so it is important to look at how those needs vary, both across many types of organisation and through the progressive development of one. In order to understand this diversity fully, the book is divided into two parts. The first part gives an introduction to board operation and describes the needs of different types of board and the roles that board members can play. It provides the background to board behaviour. The second part then focuses on the core issue of the people element of board operation. It introduces the Frame Model which defines the roles that a board needs to fulfil in order to be effective. This model provides a framework for reviewing the behaviour and interaction of board members to help identify and resolve board dynamics problems. The same model is then used to provide an insight into the dynamics of the whole organisation resulting from the board's deliberations.

The two parts of the book can be read independently. It has been structured to be used as a reference work that can be dipped into as required. This has necessitated some elements of repetition which hopefully will not cause too many issues when the whole book is read at first.

The legal and regulatory aspects of the discussion are targeted primarily at a UK audience and are subject to change. Many of the other issues that are raised are generic, including the critical issues relating to personal interaction.

Contents

Part 1 – Board functions:
How a board works

Boards are very diverse. Each board combines some common features with its own unique characteristics. It is important to understand the nature of boards, what their functions are and what roles their board members play. Part 1 provides the background and framework of board operation. If the reader is familiar with these aspects then you might wish to go straight to Part 2 which examines how people behave and interact in the board environment.

1. Introduction

Boards are groups of strong, capable people with shared goals. Their decisions dictate the direction of the organisations they control and they take full responsibility for the results that are achieved. Board dynamics are the interactions between board members and are the main focus of this book. This interaction has to be challenging in order to protect the organisation and its impact can be very significant. Before analysing board dynamics it is necessary to understand the various types of board operation as these provide the context that drives board behaviour.

Why have a board?

The large majority of organisations in the UK, including those in the public sector and charities, are registered as companies of some type. They are, therefore, bound by UK company law and must have at least one director. Other than very small companies, it is obligatory to have at least two directors and a Company Secretary. Because the principles of board behaviour apply in a broader context, even to those without the formal status of director, the term 'board member' is sometimes used to cover these situations.

Each director has major functional and legal responsibilities, including significant personal liabilities. For a large, diverse organisation it is easy to see that one person could not realistically understand all the issues that the organisation faces. Therefore, it makes sense for such organisations to have several directors who not only provide the required breadth of understanding but also help each other to ensure that nothing important is missed. This group of directors constitutes the board. Thus, a board is much more than just a collective noun for directors. The group provides a forum for understanding the organisation, the broader context of its market and the external forces that impact on it. The board can then decide how the organisation needs to behave in order to achieve its goals and protect its stakeholders. A board can be a very powerful tool, based on a team of experienced and capable individuals, delivering major benefits.

An imperative element for each and every director is that he or she is personally responsible and can be liable for any mistakes for which the board is held responsible, even if these are not in his or her area of expertise. In legal terms this is a form of 'joint and several liability'. Such shared risk means that someone who has a claim against the organisation can seek recompense from just one director rather than the whole board or the organisation. It is common practice for larger companies to have a form of insurance called 'directors' and officers' liability cover' to protect the individual directors. Such insurance only covers the individuals against proper behaviour. If directors have done something that is very unreasonable or even illegal then they are still personally liable. Shared risks and liabilities impose a major burden on the board and its members, demanding a high level of capability and mutual respect between board members.

Whilst the need for a board may be obvious for complex organisations, the same is not true for smaller businesses. It is common for them to use a minimum number of directors. Independent non-executives are a rarity. Small organisations may be very simple but the world in which they operate is not. They are subject to the same complex, economic, legal and regulatory environment and often the risks to the individual concerned are much higher. For example, if the Chief Executive Officer (CEO) of a multinational corporation makes a mistake and loses his or her job then he or she probably has a very large financial cushion as protection. At the other end of the scale, if a butcher's shop inadvertently causes food poisoning due to poor hygiene then the owners could lose not only their incomes but also their life savings and face the prospect of prosecution for breach of health and safety regulations. A board provides more pairs of eyes looking for opportunities and risks for all types of organisation, large and small. It allows the organisation to bring in strong individuals with experience who can help guide it towards its goals and helps key staff to share the burdens of leadership and responsibility. In particular, independent non-executives can bring an objective view which can be invaluable, whatever the size of the organisation.

There are other legal structures that an organisation can take, for example partnerships. Most organisations have a committee or group to steer them which faces the same issues of behaviour and personal interaction as a company board.

Board operation

The primary function of a board is to act as the guardian of an organisation. It has a duty to protect the organisation and to ensure that it performs appropriately. The board should provide an objective review of the organisation, guidance to the management team and act as an interface to stakeholders. The board has a vital role to play in the wellbeing of the organisation.

It is, therefore, essential that the board itself works effectively.

There are several well established methods for reviewing the performance and balance of management teams. However, boards have very different characteristics and styles in terms of their modus operandi and the nature of the people on the board.

There are two basic types of team operation: interdependent and independent. In the case of an interdependent team, each member of the team performs a different task which the other team members depend on. For example, this applies to football teams and to most management teams. In an independent team, each team member operates separately and the team performance is the sum of the individual performances. This applies for example to single play golf teams such as in the Ryder Cup. A board combines elements of both types of team model. It acts as an interdependent team to ensure that all key aspects of the organisation can be monitored and as an independent team since each director has personal responsibility for its decisions and needs to understand the entire scope of the organisation.

There are also two main styles of decision making: the autocratic and the consensus. It is common for people on company boards to have an autocratic style since it is often the style that elevated them to a board level position. This style is normally associated with a more aggressive, dynamic organisation and with a willingness to take and manage risks. However, decision making in a group of autocrats can be more difficult because of this aggression. Public sector boards are more likely to have a consensus style which can be more constrained and risk averse but this may make the decision making better balanced. Whatever the style, boards have collective responsibility and this makes it imperative that they make decisions as a team.

If the board is to be effective then it must be willing and able to have challenging and open discussions in order to identify potential opportunities, problems and risk areas. This requires a careful balance between the autocratic and the consensus styles because both elements are needed to achieve this objective.

Boards are committees with a very high level of personal authority and responsibility of which typically less than half, namely the executive directors of the organisation, are part of a clearly defined team. Executive directors have two very distinct roles to fill; as directors they are part of the board and as executives they are part of the management team.

The level of involvement of non-executive directors (NEDs) can vary considerably from a monitoring role in large public companies to a very hands-on role in some venture capital (VC) backed private companies. The NEDs can motivate, mentor and monitor the executives in the same way as any manager but both the scope for error and the stakes are a lot higher. The chairman has a foot in both camps because he or she is the primary link between the board and the CEO as well as being the leader of the board.

Directors are usually selected based on their experience at a high level in similar organisations. In practice, most senior managers aspire to being directors because it is seen as a mark of status. All too often in smaller organisations they are unaware of the role and responsibilities they aspire to.

Directors are often 'shapers' (in Belbin analysis (1) parlance) and have strong self-belief. These factors make the board an unbalanced team. In some boards this is not an issue but in others the personal dynamics within the board can be a major barrier to the success of the organisation. This raises the core question of how to assess the effectiveness of a board and how to choose directors to maximise the likelihood of the board working in a constructive manner.

Many directors, and in particular the large majority of NEDs, are selected from a known pool or database of individuals that are trusted by either the executives or the investors. This may look like a safe option. However, it does not take into account the effect of the individual on board dynamics. The executives and investors tend to choose someone with a similar personality to their own or whom they think is amenable to their style. This approach can inhibit the challenging discussions that are essential. New board members are usually chosen because of their specific experience without taking into account how their personality will affect board dynamics. Such constraints on the choice of board members increase the risk that board dynamics will damage the organisation's performance.

As a company develops from an initial concept to a mature business, the requirements of the board change significantly and, therefore, the board itself should also change. An example of the potentially radical nature of this evolution is highlighted in Moore's well-known book *Crossing the Chasm* (2). The more innovative the business, the more the board must adapt as the company grows. Such a progression can be anticipated from an early stage and the board members should understand that their roles form part of a progressive development. Using a planned process helps to avoid 'founder syndrome' and other issues that can occur as an organisation develops. Managing this evolution successfully can be difficult and it is important to achieve the right balance of reward between the different generations of boards and management.

A review of a recent book stated "The board activities, with egos, rivalries, game-playing and double-dealing added considerably to the length of the corporate depression. It was to take eight long years of turmoil under four chief executives before the tide of opinion began, once more, to turn in its favour" (3). The company concerned was Marks & Spencer. The story of Robert Maxwell is another classic example of how boards can fail. Sadly, there are many instances of less prestigious boards that failed to deliver, leading to serious consequences for the organisations concerned. Understanding and facing up to the issues that make a board work effectively can be a major contributor to excellent business performance. It is probably true to say that it takes a great board to make a company great and to keep it that way.

A number of examples are presented in the text in order to highlight various aspects of board behaviour. These are all based on real experience. The situations were often far more complex and, therefore, impossible to describe in a few words. They have been heavily edited to emphasise the point to be made and also to protect the identities of those involved. I hope that the parties concerned will understand and accept the need to be 'economical with the truth'.

It is important to recognise that some people whose job title includes the word 'director' are not directors in the true legal sense. In the case of UK companies, legal directors are registered at Companies House, having completed Form 288a. For example, a company which is a single legal entity may have a number of operating divisions, each of which is run by a 'Managing Director'. Unless these individuals are registered as being board members of the overall company, they are not actually directors and, therefore, theoretically do not have the same personal responsibilities and liabilities. However, if they present themselves to the outside world as a director of a legal entity then they may still be liable. In terms of the way in which people interact on a board, the distinction between legal directors and other board players is not a critical factor.

Responsibilities of board members

The responsibilities and accountability of board members have increased progressively over recent years. The days of boards being an old boys' network ended as a result of investor and media pressure followed by political pressure arising from tales of corporate mismanagement and greed. The increasing use of power by investors, especially by major financial institutions, was a very powerful tool to change the way that boards thought and how they presented themselves to the outside world. Corporate governance became a major issue, leading in the UK to the publication of the Higgs Report (4) and later documents which formed the *Combined Code on Corporate Governance* (5) issued by the Financial Reporting Council.

Stricter corporate governance did not prevent the Marconi debacle. In the US, the Enron disaster forced a radical rethink leading to the Sarbanes-Oxley rules (6). Some US firms have chosen to list on overseas markets such as the Alternative Investment Market (AIM) on the London Stock Exchange to avoid the burden and cost of

Sarbanes-Oxley compliance. Directors of non-US companies with US subsidiaries can be extradited to the US if the company has operations there. This is a very real threat, especially for directors of large corporations and many non-US companies now choose not to have subsidiaries in the US. However, being a director of US companies has become a challenging and stimulating opportunity that some people relish.

The success of AIM itself was driven by its offering a combination of public listing on a high profile market but with relatively light regulations and lower compliance cost. This has led in turn to the growth of the PLUS market which effectively undercuts AIM in terms of regulation and compliance costs. The downside of the lighter structure of these markets is the lack of liquidity because of the smaller base of investors that is comfortable with them. However, none of these factors reduce the responsibility of board members.

The result of the changes is that the individual director has much greater personal responsibility and risk. He or she has a duty to find out reasonable information about the organisation and cannot rely solely on what the executive management chooses to impart.

The board as an 'unbalanced team'

When venture capital and private equity investors look at a new opportunity, their assessment of the management team is a critical element of their due diligence and it is common for them to insist on psychometric tests of the team to confirm their views. They clearly recognise the importance of the team and the individual personalities. However, it is uncommon for them to undertake a similar review of the board even though the interaction of their appointed directors and the management team can be at least as important as that within the management team itself. Such investor organisations prefer to use their own staff or people from a highly experienced pool, all of whom may regard themselves as professional directors who can operate effectively in any investee company. Whilst this might be true, it fails to recognise the detrimental effect that their appointed director(s) can sometimes have on the operation of the board as a team.

A board by its very nature is almost always a group of strong-minded individuals who have made their mark sufficiently to make a meaningful contribution as board members. They are more likely to be leaders and visionaries than team players and, therefore, the board becomes an unbalanced team. For some aspects of board operation this may not be a problem but for others it clearly is. For example, when reviewing the strategy that is presented by the CEO and executive team, the board relies on the complementary skills of the board members and their ability to work cohesively to achieve an effective and thorough review. This is difficult to do if all the board members are jostling for position as leaders. In contrast, sometimes the most effective form of risk identification is when individuals use their insight and knowledge to spot potential weaknesses. The key difference between these two examples is that the former is trying to make sure that the strategy is coherent whereas the latter is looking for cracks and flaws in the system or proposal.

An unbalanced team can be used to create a constructive tension that can be very effective (Example 1). The risk is that the interaction between strong individuals works to the detriment of the board and this is one of the key themes of the second part of this book.

Example 1

The CEO of a multinational listed group was concerned that the interaction between his senior team, comprising the key corporate staff and the divisional Managing Directors (MDs), was confrontational rather than constructive. He brought all the key staff to a workshop run by an external facilitator to find a way forward. The facilitator asked everyone to do a psychometric test that purported to identify their main characteristic and how strong it was. One of the characteristics was 'dominance' and the maximum level was seven. Every single member of the team came out as a 'dominant 7'. The organisation had been set up to give full authority and responsibility to this group of individuals and there was always an element of competition between the divisions of the group. The conflict was a direct result.

The group needed strong people in these roles. However, the assessment process made the individuals far more aware of themselves and their peers. The interaction between them improved directly as a result. The outcome demonstrates the importance not only of being self-aware but also aware of critical relationships with others, in particular where they are peer-level power relationships. Because the whole team was assessed at the same time, it was much easier to share the information and the assessment was not considered threatening by anyone involved.

Objectivity of board review

The burden of responsibility for ensuring effective board performance lies with the board itself. In particular, the chairman must take the lead role as his or her primary responsibility is to manage the board. A key issue is that understanding the impact of board dynamics requires a high degree of objectivity because the board members themselves may be part of the problem.

Such issues are compounded by the likelihood that the directors are strong characters who regard their own views and approach as correct. Their belief can increase the more they are challenged. Sometimes this is an essential characteristic, for example, in order to counter 'group think' and to be able to challenge other members of the board. However, it is important for the other members of the board to be able to recognise when a vigorous pursuit of the truth crosses the line into dogmatism.

In contrast, weak directors are potentially far more dangerous to a board because they are unable or unwilling to provide a constructive challenge. They can be targeted by strong board members to align with them in an argument. The balance between adequate strength and potential conflict is difficult but is necessary to achieve. A combination of thorough director selection and effective chairmanship are the primary enabling tools.

Successful boards

Successful boards have three core features:

- A collection of abilities that can effectively address the needs and aspirations of the organisation
- The ability to communicate effectively as a group to ensure that all significant issues are raised and discussed properly
- The willingness to challenge and be challenged so that key areas are addressed rigorously and that any disagreements are constructive.

The three features interact with each other. In particular, poor communication may well mean that the board's abilities are not being utilised and that disagreements become conflicts. The impact of poor communication is further emphasised by the dichotomy of board structures, with executives and non-executives.

The executive directors work together as part of the management team. Therefore, they must communicate well with each other if they are to make any progress. Such interaction is essential but it must not be exclusive otherwise there is a strong risk of 'group think'. The non-executive directors meet mainly in the formal situation of board meetings which places a significant burden on the chairman to ensure that the non-executives interact effectively with the board as a whole.

The chairman must have a very strong and clear communication link to the CEO. This acts as a bridge between one as the leader of both the board and the non-executives and the other as the leader of the management team. It should also be used to ensure that the executives understand the difference between their roles as executives and their roles as directors.

Key influences

The key influences are different at various stages in the development of the organisation and there is a series of key questions that need to be asked to check these (Figure 1):

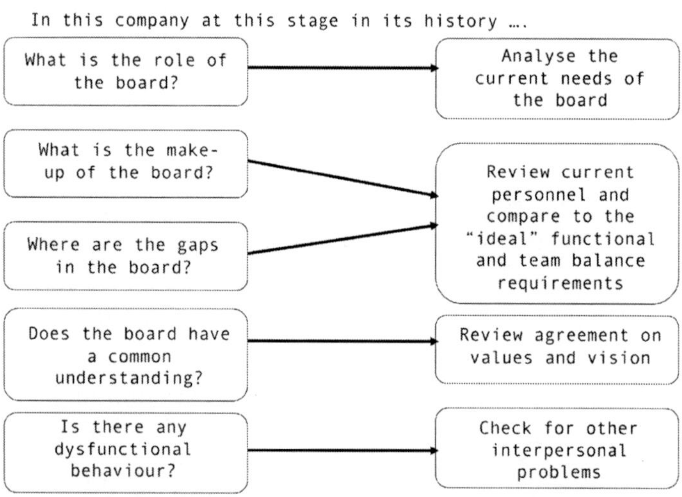

Figure 1

The common features of successful boards are centred on their ability both to identify the major influences that will affect the future of the organisation and to ensure that the organisation is fully prepared to minimise the risks and maximise the opportunities associated with these influences. This means that the structure and operation of the organisation, the executive team and the board itself need to be able to adapt to changing circumstances.

Sometimes the major influences are long-term, for example market and technology trends where the board requires the vision to understand and appreciate these trends. Their interpretation enables the organisation to gain competitive advantage based on its unique vision. Sometimes the influences appear rapidly, as with an accident, the recruitment of a key member of staff or the impact of the economic crisis that started in 2008. Whilst any sound organisation will have contingency plans in place to react to such influences, they need different types of reaction from the board to ensure that the organisation is protected as effectively as possible and is in a position to implement appropriate plans. Such a risk-focused approach aims to guide the organisation through the new minefield.

The board needs to have both breadth of experience to address a range of eventualities and breadth of personality types. In the examples given above, the visionary strategic thinker who can identify and plan the exploitation of long-term trends is unlikely to be good at reacting to short-term crises. The converse is also true. Furthermore, mixing individuals who are sufficiently different to be able to guide the board through these different eventualities raises the potential of personality conflict because their viewpoints are so distinct. A good board achieves good interaction between a diverse group of strong individuals who respect each other's opinions and are willing to question and be questioned without generating conflict (Example 2).

Example 2

The executive chairman of a multinational public company, who had built the business, had an ongoing difference of opinion with the other executive directors about the strategic direction of the company. A downturn in the global market brought matters to a head. When a board vote became necessary to resolve this, the non-executive directors had a side meeting and decided to support the executive directors against the chairman. The chairman resigned immediately. He left both the board meeting and the company to a stunned silence from the rest of the board. The senior non-executive, who was normally relatively quiet, then took charge. He said "we have lost chairmen before" and took control of the meeting. One of the other non-executives was elected chairman and the meeting continued. The balance and mutual respect in the board thereby avoided a major hiatus that could have been seriously damaging to the company.

This is a good example not only of a balanced board that would not let itself be dominated by a particularly strong individual but also of non-executive directors working in a very effective way to protect the greater interests of the company.

An effective board combines clear vision and understanding of future options with a sound approach to risk management. Under normal circumstances, the former is the key factor that separates truly successful organisations. On some occasions, the latter becomes the critical issue and it can have a major impact on the survival of the organisation.

2. Types of board

Boards take a number of forms, ranging from company boards to boards of governors and partnership committees, depending on the type of organisation. Every board has a number of members, usually including both executives and non-executives. Some boards are formed exclusively of one or the other. Board members have significant personal legal responsibilities when the organisation concerned is, as is usually the case, a legal entity. In effect, the organisation is considered in legal terms to be a person and the board is the guardian of that person.

Most board members are legal directors of the organisation. Some boards have 'observers' who attend and contribute to board meetings but do not vote. UK law does allow for people who are not legally directors to be regarded as having full legal responsibilities, called 'shadow directors', which is a risk for observers and others. Some organisations have a separate advisory board or council which supports the main board but whose members do not share the full legal responsibilities of the main board.

The boards that receive the greatest attention, particularly in respect of corporate governance, are those of large corporate companies. However, in most countries the legal responsibilities of directors of incorporated entities are essentially the same for all organisations, irrespective of the size of the company or whether they are private sector companies or public sector bodies. They are still subject to scrutiny and potential litigation by all stakeholders.

A partnership is a common alternative to a company as a legal structure, especially for professional groups such as lawyers or accountants. Whilst partnerships work in a different way, the importance of board dynamics remains the same and they both have the extra motivation of joint and several liability if things go wrong.

The boards of governors of public sector bodies, such as hospitals, universities and schools, have significant responsibilities coupled with very high levels of public accountability. These create different but equally challenging roles. Whereas private sector and company boards are focused primarily on shareholders who are regarded as the key subset of their stakeholders, public sector boards are focused on their overall group of stakeholders, thereby changing the balance and dynamics.

Public company boards

Public company boards are subject to the rules of the stock exchange in which they operate as well as the standard legal framework and, because of the nature of their shareholder base, are subject to much wider scrutiny.

There is a running game between the directors of public companies and their shareholders. Investor relations are a primary task for the CEO, Chief Financial Officer (CFO) and chairman. Major institutional shareholders and analysts will expect, and get, regular updates from board members but the company is not allowed to say something to one shareholder that it does not say to all. Significant events have to be formally notified to the stock exchange, which then makes it public, usually on its web site and through news services. The shareholders want a prediction of performance that the directors are not permitted to give them so the analysts do this under the guidance of the company because the company would have to announce if it disagreed with the forecast.

These requirements have a major impact on the board dynamics and the types of people who are suitable to be board members. The directors who deal with investor relations must have excellent communication skills and personal credibility. This augurs well for effective board dynamics but it is counterbalanced by the scale of the returns. The latter might make some directors more focused on personal gain than is good for the organisation.

The Enron and Marconi debacles have forced increasing regulation and accountability in this arena. This is further supported by more active institutional investors who often take a very keen interest in corporate governance as well as financial performance. They also look at the personal performance of directors and will put pressure on those that they feel are not up to the mark. The reaction to this can be a show of strength from the directors concerned which in turn leads to an emphasis on their own performance rather than that of the business.

The increased pressures on directors in this sector have reduced the number of people who might consider taking on these roles. This has happened at the same time that leading organisations have been deliberately trying to find new blood to work on these boards.

Subsidiary company boards

The boards of subsidiary companies are often very small and only have executives as directors. Executives of the parent companies effectively take on the role of non-executives in the subsidiaries. Formal board meetings can be rare, with board meetings convened on an ad hoc basis to formalise the decisions and processes defined by the directors in their executive roles. The board in this case is a close knit team. However, being too close can create issues, particularly as the reporting hierarchy inherent in the team can stifle open debate on key issues.

For most practical purposes, having such a small board can be very effective but the directors still have their full legal responsibilities and can be called to account not just by the parent company but by other stakeholders, especially the employees. A number of regulatory issues, such as health and safety, make these directors vulnerable if reasonable corporate governance has not been seen to be practised.

The MD of the subsidiary should be the driving force behind the company. It is very important that this role is balanced by someone, normally the Finance Director (FD), who is strong enough to stand up to the MD and is willing to take issues to the parent company if required.

Subsidiary boards can become very challenging for international operations where the foreign directors from the parent company may have little understanding of the different legal framework in which they are operating. These responsibilities can ripple back up to the main board directors. This has become a major issue for US companies with their aggressive corporate regulations. For example, a partner from a leading British recruitment company has advised candidates not only not to take a non-executive role for a US company but also not to take one for a company with a US subsidiary because the risks are too high for the returns that a non-executive receives.

It is not uncommon for the executives of subsidiary companies, or even divisions, to be given the title of director when they are not registered as such at Companies House. In practice they can be seen as shadow directors and the companies need to be aware of the risks this creates, especially if others believe that these individuals have made decisions on behalf of the business as legal directors.

Private company boards

Private companies have become even more significant in recent years due to the increase in major private equity deals taking public companies back into private hands. Traditional private companies of all sizes were typically owned by a closed group of founders and their families and descendants, with the ownership spreading to other classes of investors as the company developed. This still applies to many companies but those that need greater levels of funding, which cannot be financed by the closed group or through debt, have turned to business angels, venture capital or private equity according to the level of funding they require.

The boards of family-owned businesses have a unique dynamic that combines the normal operations of a board with the emotional interaction that ties a family together but can also drive it apart. Sometimes the interaction is very constructive, especially in the early stages of the company although it may deteriorate as the company matures. It can be difficult to bring in outsiders into a family board because, by definition, they are excluded from some of the issues. However, it is very important to do so as it is easy for a family board to lack objectivity and the breadth of experience to tackle new issues. A non-family director can overcome these issues but it requires a particular type of person to be effective in such a role.

Business angels, venture capitalists and private equity companies are typically very active investors, often insisting on a board position to monitor their investment and to help the management. They all have preferred market sectors in which they operate and it is usually their sector specialist who gets put on the board, irrespective of personal style (Example 3). Even without personality clashes, there can be conflicts because the investors can be interested in optimising their portfolio rather than optimising the investee company. This is usually highlighted in their approach to risk management. If the investor sees the investee as a 'banker' then he or she may wish to take a more conservative approach than the investee. If the investee is seen as having the potential for star returns then the investor may push for a more aggressive approach than the investee would naturally take.

Example 3

A venture capital company, which was the lead investor in an early stage technology company, was considering a further round of investment. Despite the fact that it had been actively involved in the company for several years, it insisted on a full due diligence, including psychometric testing for the management team as it felt there were problems within.

The management team came out as being very well balanced. The CEO told the person doing the psychometric testing that the only issue was a personality clash between himself and the director from the VC firm. The tester had assessed the VC director prior to his recruitment by the VC and had found him to be very difficult to work with but the VC chose to ignore this.

In due course, the clash between the CEO and the VC director came to its inevitable conclusion with the departure of the CEO. Thereafter the VC director took very tight control of the management team and the company performance foundered, in part due to the imbalance he created.

This reflects the irony of an investor being very concerned about the dynamics of the management team but not applying the same logic to the board as a team, despite having full information available. It is not unusual for investor organisations to take this attitude whereas a more balanced approach that recognises their role as part of the board team could be much more effective and, therefore, deliver greater returns.

The same issue applies in family businesses where the main shareholder may see the business as his or her pension fund and, therefore, be more risk averse than would benefit the business. The counter to this is to demonstrate the conflict of interest to the shareholder. It can be much harder to get this accepted than might be thought, especially if there are no independent directors on the board. Conflict of interest is an important issue in many boards but it can be particularly serious for private companies.

Partnerships

Many organisations find that a partnership or limited liability partnership can be the most effective way to run their businesses. This applies particularly to professional service companies such as lawyers, architects or accountants.

Such organisations usually have management committees or partners' committees which take the place of the board. Members of these 'boards' have similar levels of responsibility to directors but with a more explicit emphasis on the burden of joint and several liability.

Lawyer and accountancy partnerships frequently do not have people with management training and experience. The level of management and co-ordination that is required in these businesses is much lower than in other organisations because they are essentially independent teams rather than interdependent teams. However, the risk levels are not different, as the collapse of the major accountancy firm, Arthur Andersen, in 2002 demonstrated and the 'board' has the responsibility for managing these risks.

A core question in such partnerships is how does someone get to be Managing Partner? There is often pressure to appoint the highest fee earner but this reduces his or her earning capacity. Such people may also be the least inclined to become administrative managers. It is important that the partnership is wary of confusing the expert role with that of the professional leader and board member. An understanding of risk management should be a key criterion in such appointments.

Charity boards – the third sector

Charities range from very large, complex international organisations with huge budgets to very small operations. In this respect they reflect the same broad scope as businesses. The boards of charities were historically staffed by altruistic people who often had in depth experience of running other organisations, both from the public and private sectors. Whilst the board members typically sat on other boards, the organisations were normally quite traditional in their approach. Two changes in the sources of funding have changed this approach.

The National Lottery started in the UK in 1994 with a remit to distribute 28% of its revenues to 'good causes'. This channelled a very significant proportion of charitable donations through a single organisation. Accessing this source of funds became highly competitive. At the same time, a number of very generous but entrepreneurial benefactors took the view that their charitable donations ought to be managed as effectively as any other investment they made. The charities needed to demonstrate how effective they were in their use of funds to increase their chances of getting access to them.

The result has been that the charities, and in particular their executive teams, have become much more business-like in their operations. The pay for executives has increased to attract higher quality individuals and the board pressures reflect both the more competitive environment and the need to be seen to be effective fund managers. The outcome is that the difference between a charity and a business in terms of the demands on, and operation of, its board is now relatively small.

Public sector boards

The majority of public sector bodies in the UK are incorporated. Therefore, the board members have the same responsibilities, liabilities and accountability as for any other company. It is quite common for such organisations to also have a council of governors acting as advisory boards with a much broader membership.

Public life in the UK is theoretically governed by seven principles – selflessness, integrity, objectivity, accountability, openness, honesty and leadership. Apart from constraints on the openness for reasons of commercial sensitivity, these are very good principles for any director, especially if selflessness is replaced by 'acting in the best interests of the organisation'. Indeed, it would be sensible to challenge any director who does not adequately reflect these seven principles.

Public sector organisations have a different motivation to commercial enterprises. They are driven by broader stakeholder interest and not just shareholder interest. In the UK they normally have, either directly or with the council of governors, a good representation of the stakeholders, leading to relatively large boards. As is common in group behaviour, larger groups can stifle discussion and creativity. For example, it is commonly believed that the best group size for a brainstorming session is from six to eight people – below this it is too easy for some members to dominate and above this some group members become wary of expressing their opinions.

Increasingly, public sector boards are seeking people with commercial experience to provide a broader base of experience. Bodies such as universities and large hospitals have annual budgets of tens or hundreds of millions of pounds. They need to be sure that these funds are managed in a commercially astute manner.

Whilst the sizes of the budgets are often those of a large commercial organisation, the motivation of the board members is usually different. Although the remuneration of senior public sector executives is on a par with the private sector, membership of boards of governors is frequently either low paid or unpaid. Such roles attract particular types of individual, i.e. those with a strong social or political conscience, or people who represent the interests of a particular stakeholder. This gives a greater scope for conflict between the executive directors and the NEDs.

The twist in the public sector is that the guidelines and operating conditions for such organisations are commonly set by local or national politicians who may also determine the way in which the organisations are funded. This puts a major constraint on the organisation and the board. Whilst these conditions might be used as a 'get out clause' for the board, they do nothing to protect the personal positions and reputations of the board members with their stakeholders or their political masters. The board members are truly caught between a rock and a hard place.

The political dimension means that these boards are likely to take a consensus approach, if only from the principle of 'safety in numbers'. However, when there is a strong political presence on the board, a change in the political balance can lead to shifts in policy to reflect those of the strongest group. Such shifts raise the question of who is in control of the organisation, the board or the political party?

Public sector boards are very diverse. One example is given below to highlight some of the specific issues that such organisations face.

University boards of governors – leading an education business

It is increasingly common for private sector organisations to get a significant element of their income from customers so they have a foot in both the public and private sector camps. Universities are such an example. The top tier universities have global reputations to maintain and they attract students and staff from around the world. Some of the lower tier universities have a strong emphasis on overseas students because their fee income helps to offset the relatively poor research funding that such institutions attract.

As a result of the financial and market pressures, many UK universities are becoming increasingly aware of their competitive position both nationally and internationally. Therefore, they are now facing marketing issues that are not unfamiliar to large private sector companies. They face similar problems in achieving the right balance between research (=development) and teaching (=production) and are considering outsourcing non-core activities such as facilities. Both elements are key sources of funding, particularly as governmental funding for research is linked to the perceived quality of the university's research profile. The financial pressure that this creates forces less well established universities to put a major emphasis on commercial funding for research and vocationally-oriented courses, making them far more like normal business operations. The ability of the university to build relationships with and influence its main funding sources becomes critical to its success in the same way that a company needs to manage its key customers.

In common with most public sector organisations, a large part of the funding comes directly from government and most of the remainder is heavily influenced by government policy. Government also defines the rules by which such organisations operate so whilst the funding may be more predictable than for commercial organisations, the ability to influence it is considerably less. This constrains the scope of the board in managing the organisation, replacing the challenges faced by commercial companies with other no less challenging issues.

In most respects, universities are now education businesses but with a different ulterior motive. The stakeholder dimension means that the boards of governors may be much larger than company boards. Increased size makes it more difficult to effect significant changes because it introduces more inertia into the system. As a result, major changes tend to be imposed by external factors. The base of power then shifts to the operating committees where more normal rules of board dynamics apply.

Board committees

Boards have a wide range of issues to consider, some of which benefit from specialist knowledge. It is common for the boards of complex organisations to form committees to look at specific areas in detail using board members who have expertise in that area. The three most common types of committee are: audit, nominations and remuneration.

Audit committees focus on the control, monitoring and risk factors associated with financial management.

The committee is normally chaired by a non-executive with a sound knowledge of accounting and financial practice and includes the CFO and selected non-executives.

The nominations committee is responsible for finding new board members to cover the planned replacement of non-executives at the end of their terms of office. It is common practice for the committee to maintain a list of candidates for non-executive and, sometimes, executive positions in case someone leaves unexpectedly or needs to be replaced. The nominations committee usually comprises the chairman, the senior non-executive and other non-executives. The committee may seek input from the CEO but he or she is not normally a formal member of the committee.

The remuneration committee is made up exclusively of non-executives. Its primary role is to ensure that the rewards for the executive team are appropriate to the nature of the organisation and that the structure reflects the agreed goals. The remuneration package needs to have the right balance between short-term and long-term incentives and motivate the executives to take a level of risk that is suitable for the organisation. The committee also sets the remuneration for the non-executives, i.e. they set their own pay. They must be seen to do this in an objective and impartial manner so they often seek advice from specialist external advisers and from the main stakeholders.

Board committees are simply subsets of the board. They do not make decisions in their own right, even though they might be quorate in terms of the whole board. They must present their findings and recommendations to the whole board for approval before any action can be taken.

3. The roles of the board

The key roles of the board effectively split into two dimensions:

- the universal responsibilities that arise because of the legal and regulatory obligations of the board and its members and that any shareholder would reasonably expect of any board
- the specific responsibilities that arise because of the way that the organisation and the board choose to interact.

Some of the detailed responsibilities are outlined in Figure 2. These roles are underpinned by factors that influence the organisation. Most of them, including the issues of the environment (in the broader sense) and the market are outside the control of the board but are things of which it needs to be very conscious. The experience of the executive team is under the control of the board but is often a compromise between having critical and specialist skills and having broader experience.

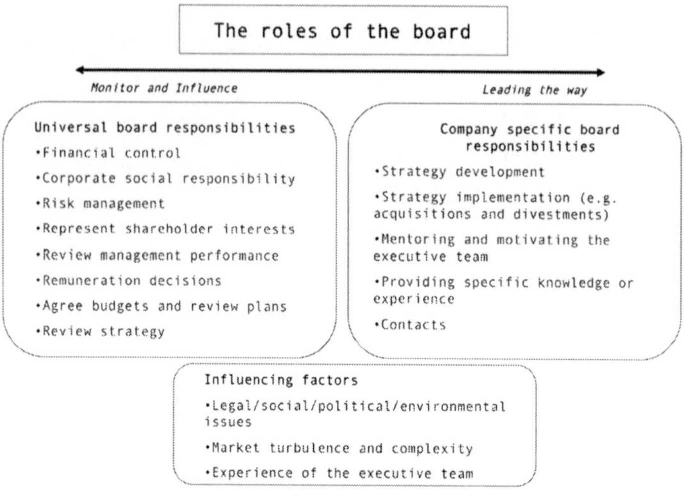

Figure 2

The board has a diverse range of responsibilities that requires a multi-faceted approach. The universal board responsibilities cover four main areas:

- managing the future – markets, strategy and budgets
- managing risk – including financial control, turbulence, legal and political
- operational issues – monitoring, mentoring and rewarding management and the workforce
- external interfaces – shareholder interests and corporate social responsibility (CSR).

A board needs to act as both poacher and gamekeeper in that it is responsible for ensuring that the organisation delivers the performance its stakeholders expect whilst monitoring the company to ensure that it is operating in an appropriate manner and in accordance with good corporate governance practice. This duality is reflected in the balance between the executive and the non-executive directors and guarantees a level of tension in the board's operation. The high levels of personal responsibility and reward serve to increase the tension further.

Capable, calm, analytical individuals make good board members but they may lack the vision necessary to take an organisation forward. Creative visionaries add real value but also generate conflict leading to challenging board dynamics, especially in start-up organisations. A major problem that many companies face as they grow is the 'founder syndrome' where the creative founder remains on the board, often with a significant shareholding, when the company has matured to a stage that no longer requires his or her particular style. The board should be seen as team that evolves in parallel with the company and one where individual directors accept that they have a limited period of usefulness.

Despite the goal of having objectivity, many board members will have a bias because they are part of, or are linked to, a power group, e.g. the executive team or a major shareholder. There is sometimes a difficult line to be drawn between the board's responsibility to represent shareholder interests and those of a specific shareholder. Changes in corporate governance have recognised the problems that this creates and have increased pressure on public companies to appoint independent directors who are truly impartial both in terms of their alignment and their motivation, for example, by not having share options. This is often difficult in SMEs but is less common than it should be, especially in smaller public companies. The problem becomes acute in family-owned businesses, where some sources suggest that only a quarter have directors who are not from the family, making it very difficult for them to be truly objective.

Corporate governance

The main challenge of corporate governance is to ensure that the risks and challenges that the organisation faces are fully understood and are managed effectively. This must be done in an open and transparent manner.

Risk assessment

A critical issue for a board is how to recognise a problem in the organisation. There are a number of key questions that need to be answered.

- Do the executives have a good understanding of the details?
- Are the executives open about issues with the NEDs?
- Who on the board sees the bigger picture risks, e.g. political, legal, economic, environmental, social and technological (PLEEST)? Sometimes ethical is added to the list and the acronym becomes STEEPLE.
- Who understands the market and the competition?

Financial controls form a key part of risk management. The metrics that lie behind financial controls provide historical information whereas effective risk management demands that warning information is received as soon as possible. The topic of metrics is discussed in more detail in Chapter 8. The board needs to ensure that the organisation has systems and communication channels in place to provide an early warning of potentially serious risk areas.

The nature of risk changes as organisations become more sophisticated. A paper by Williams, Bertsch et al (7) outlines three levels of risk:

- Those that will happen
- Those that might happen but are rare
- Those that are not expected at all.

Organisations that do not have processes to manage the first level will not survive very long. Good organisations have processes in place to manage the second level. Managing the third requires a very different management approach and different types of manager who accept the likelihood of failure and then fix the resulting issues. This is more than fire-fighting because the risks that were not expected at all frequently come from areas with which the organisation is unfamiliar and so require managers who can assimilate new information quickly and react to them in what may be a crisis situation.

In a small organisation and when the cost of getting things wrong may be relatively low then it is not too much of a problem. For large, complex organisations it can become a very serious issue because the scope for unforeseen risk areas is higher. However, risk is relative not absolute: a lesser problem may have a much more damaging effect on a small business than a greater one has on a large business.

Managing this third level risk is the domain of world class companies. It is also a major threat to many innovative companies, including start-ups, which often lack the experience to overcome the challenge. Businesses that are pushing the boundaries of technology or creating new markets are very vulnerable to the most challenging level of risk because they operate in novel and, therefore, unpredictable areas.

The third level of risk can be addressed using techniques such as scenario planning which is a tool used by some organisations to develop flexible long-term plans. It is based on classic methods used by military intelligence and was developed for business by companies like Royal Dutch Shell plc. Scenario planning is a technique for learning about the future by understanding the nature and impact of the most uncertain and important driving forces affecting our world. In this way, risks may be sometimes anticipated or their impact minimized (8).

Perceptions of risk

A common issue in risk assessment is agreeing what constitutes an acceptable level of commercial risk. The 'credit crunch' that started in 2008 was a dramatic example. It demonstrated that risks can be underestimated on a global scale, even with some superb intellects assessing those risks. Different individuals have very different views about what constitutes a risk and this can become critical in innovative ventures. It is very easy for 'group think' to make organisations underestimate the risks they are taking.

Technology start-ups provide a good example. Technology entrepreneurs know that things will go wrong in these businesses and the markets generally understand that their level of predictability, particularly in respect of timing, can be poor. It is commonplace for technology entrepreneurs to have too much confidence in their own invention because their vision tells them that any perceived risk is smaller than it really is, thereby increasing the overall risk level to the business significantly.

However, without the belief that problems and risks can be swept away, many technology start-ups would never develop into mature businesses.

Shadow directors

There is a level of personal risk that can arise for individuals or organisations who are not board members. If those individuals or organisations influence the company as if they were legal directors of the company, then they can be regarded in law as shadow directors with all the legal responsibilities of a director – the board equivalent of a common-law spouse.

The concept of shadow directors was designed originally to prevent people who had been struck off as directors acting as a director behind the scenes. It has now taken on a much wider meaning. For example, it can be a major issue for banks if a company breaches covenants and the bank pushes too hard to get the company to take the remedial actions that it wants. It can also be an issue for consultants or interim managers who need to take clear steps to ensure that they are not seen to guide the board or the company if it is in serious trouble.

The issue also arises in family-owned companies where only family members sit on the board but they employ outsiders in a senior management role, particularly as a general manager. In such a case, the outsiders are probably shadow directors, despite the family's wish to maintain legal control.

Differences in national legal frameworks and styles

The legal and regulatory frameworks that define the responsibilities of boards vary significantly between countries and vary according to the type of company, e.g. from a small private company to a major quoted company. The forces of globalisation mean that there has been a strong trend towards increasing the accountability of boards in the light of major corporate scandals from 2001 onwards.

The timing for the increase in accountability varies from country to country. The UK has been progressively tightening the rules of corporate governance since the late 1980s. The US lagged behind but has now developed a very stringent environment, triggered by the Enron debacle and other issues.

The Combined Code as a benchmark for the UK

The now superseded Department of Trade & Industry (DTI) in the UK initiated a series of reports over a long period on different aspects of corporate governance. These are now generally known by the name of the primary author and include:

- Greenbury – directors' service contracts and compensation
- Cadbury – reporting functions
- Higgs (4) – the role of non-executives
- Turnbull (9) – internal controls
- Smith (10) – audit committees
- Tyson (11) – broader talent pools

Recommendations from these reports were consolidated into the Financial Reporting Council's *The Combined Code on Corporate Governance* (5) which has been re-issued on a number of occasions, most recently in June 2008. The DTI's *Building Better Boards* (12) was issued in December 2004. Whilst these documents are targeted at FTSE 250 companies, they provide a very useful benchmark for all UK boards.

The UK government has been wary of forcing rules of behaviour on boards but has set clear guidelines, with regulatory support where necessary. These have been effective because of the strong pressure that has been exerted by the investment community working through bodies such as the Association of British Insurers (ABI) who represent a major body of institutional investors.

The failings in risk management within major financial institutions that were a significant factor behind the 'credit crunch' in 2008 have triggered a new review of the Combined Code. Ironically, some major banks whose risk management failed had devoted large parts of their annual reports to demonstrating how seriously they took corporate governance and the edicts of the Combined Code. Critics have pointed out that the Code can focus companies on ticking the boxes rather than on implementing the spirit of the Code.

German style boards v operating committees

Different countries have taken different approaches to resolving the potential conflict of interest between directors and executives. The boards of major British companies try to achieve this by having large boards. Major German companies often take another approach by separating the roles into two tiers. The board is the first tier and is the main authority. However, it often has no executives on it. The second tier is a management committee which supports the board. This committee comprises the executives who can make presentations to the board. This can lead to a more conservative approach because executives may be more aggressive in their solutions, as they feel they are more familiar with the issues and the risks involved, but this structure takes them out of board-level decision making. Germany's relative resilience in the credit crunch is in part a reflection of this conservative approach.

It is interesting to note that the updates in 2007 to the UK Companies Act place an increasing emphasis on conflicts of interests for individuals on the board. This may lead to more companies adopting the German model.

Impact of Sarbanes-Oxley

After the Enron scandal and other issues highlighting the lack of accountability in US corporations, the US government took rapid and strong action to put itself at the forefront of corporate governance, albeit at the price of flexibility. It introduced the *Public Company Accounting Reform and Investor Protection Act of 2002*, which is commonly called Sarbanes-Oxley. It set stringent standards for board responsibility, accountability and financial controls for all US public companies and their accounting advisers.

One result has been that a number of smaller US companies looked for Initial Placement Offerings (IPOs) on the UK's AIM market, because of the lower level of regulation and cost of compliance, whereas previously they would have gone straight to NASDAQ or the American Stock Exchange. Another result is that fewer people are willing to take directorships for US companies because of the significant increase in personal liability.

Whilst these results may not all be a direct outcome of the Sarbanes-Oxley regulations, the introduction of this rigorous regime has had a major impact on the perception of the business climate in the USA.

Matching the needs of the organisation

The nature of a board needs to reflect the circumstances of the organisation it oversees both in terms of the type of people the board requires and in its detailed processes. These circumstances then become major drivers of the board dynamics and set the requirements for the evolution of the board.

Industry type & drivers

It is self-evident that, for example, the type of people on the board of a traditional engineering company will be very different from those for an internet retailer of high fashion, but should it be? Both of these environments may be subject to huge rates of change, the latter because it is the nature of their business and the former because it needs to change rapidly to regain lost ground in a dynamic and increasingly global industry. The rate of change may be a greater factor than the industry itself in its impact on the style required from the board. The core difference in this example is that the former company is less likely to accept the importance of the industry dynamics.

The nature and style of a board normally reflect where the organisation is coming from rather than where it is going to. The executives' experience will typically have been either with the organisation itself or with similar ones because they need to be familiar with the details of the operation. The same usually applies to non-executives but it need not. There is a strong argument for bringing in non-executives who have backgrounds and experience which reflect where the organisation wants to go (Example 4). Often this experience needs to be drawn from outside the industry sector but the inherent conservatism of many boards precludes this.

Example 4

The new CEO of a multi-billion pound company in the UK wanted to change the business model from being a traditional engineering business to a support services company with a focus on the same customer base. Given the long history of the group, this vision met with a lot of resistance from parts of the board. With the support of the major shareholders, the board was restructured and the company was able to grow strongly based on its new business model.

Market conditions

Market conditions are a major determinant of the way an organisation needs to behave. Strong market growth provides conditions for rapid expansion with an emphasis on increasing resources and production, thereby driving up cash consumption. Recession leads to increased cost competition, downsizing and consolidation. Where these are medium to long-term trends, they should be reflected in the skill base and style of the board.

Most boards are reasonably equipped to deal with the normal short and medium term cyclicality of markets. Where there is a major but rare market hiatus, e.g. a global recession, then it is less likely that any board member will have first-hand experience of how to deal with the situation. High growth businesses are particularly vulnerable in these circumstances and they are the least likely to have board members who are skilled in dealing with a downturn as this does not fit in with their business model. It is always sensible for a board to know someone, such as a turn-round specialist, to whom they can turn for advice and support in the event that the market turns against them.

Maturity of the company

The issues that organisations face change significantly as they develop from start-up to maturity:

- The start-up phase is dominated by development of the prototype products or services, establishing networks and obtaining funding
- The next pre-revenue phase focuses on building market access channels, establishing production and supply chains and, once again, obtaining funding
- The core issues in the early revenue phase are competitive positioning, building a customer base, implementing the expansion strategy and funding growth
- The mature phase is broadly based and includes elements of consolidation, renewal and reinvention.

The risk levels and the nature of the risk change in response to the development of the company. The nature of the board needs to change to reflect the stage of the company, with early stages requiring more entrepreneurial approaches and the mature stages requiring a more reflective approach. A classic example of this is given in Moore's *Crossing the Chasm* model (2) which describes the hazardous route for taking a novel technology from concept to full market acceptance.

The breadth required by the board members increases if the company needs to change more rapidly, making it more difficult to find people with the right skill and experience for the task. In many respects, this reflects Maslow's hierarchy of needs (13) where the basic drive for the company to survive dominates its early stages.

It is logical that some members of the management team and the board should change in a timely and planned progression during the evolution of the company. When this does happen, it is frequently done in an unplanned and confrontational manner and is associated with the stigma of failure rather than one of using the right people at the right time. This issue is discussed in detail in Chapter 9.

It is interesting to note that there can be strong differences between the US and the UK in terms of investment approach as an organisation matures. In the US, investors are more focused on specific stages of development of their investee companies. Later stage investors in the US are happy to buy out early stage investors, allowing them to take their profits. In the UK, later stage investors normally prefer the early stage investors to stay with the company on the basis that if it is a good deal then they will want to keep their investment in the company. The downside of the UK approach is that early stage funds are not released quickly for re-investment thereby reducing the funds available for other early stage ventures. These approaches to investment are reflected in the nature of the boards of the investee businesses.

Strength of management

There is never an argument for having a weak board but it is important that the board is not so strong it does not allow the executive management team to work effectively on a day to day basis. There may be reasons for allowing a number of executive directors who are otherwise weak, provided they bring vital skills or experience to the board. For example, this can occur in start-ups where the inventor of the concept, who is often the founder of the company, may be outstandingly creative but a weak manager.

Such inventors often have an unwavering belief in the validity of their business concept and a lack of understanding of what makes a good manager. The role of the other board members is then to provide the missing skills and support the rest of the management team without stifling the creativity that provides the main impetus of the company.

A much more difficult situation arises when one individual, usually the CEO or chairman, is domineering. Such ego-driven people may force the selection of weak 'yes-men' as non-executives so they can control the board. This requires a very strong balancing force to ensure that the shareholders interests are fully taken into account and to keep the domineering director on the 'straight and narrow'.

What the board needs

The members of the board, between them, should provide:

- Personal attributes:
  - Credibility (in the eyes of stakeholders)
  - Drive and energy
  - Vision
  - Decisiveness
  - Independence
  - Impartiality
  - Insight
  - Reflection
  - Openness
  - Dignity
  - Strong interpersonal skills
  - Someone, preferably the chairman, needs to be a bridge-builder
- Knowledge:
  - Market knowledge (or know where to get it)
  - Product knowledge
  - Financial knowledge
  - Contacts
  - Skills:
    - Analytical skills (to spot problems early)
    - Interrogation skills (to probe as deeply as possible without threatening).

A key issue for board members is how much information to ask for in order to be confident that they understand what is driving the company and the risks that are involved. Too little information increases the risks but too much may slow down the process and undermine the control of the executives. The NED's dilemma may be paraphrased as 'to question or not to question, that is the question'.

Choice of board members

Often there is not a free choice of the members of the team. Individuals may be there because of their position, their knowledge or to represent a specific investor or group of investors. Where a director represents an institutional investor, the investor often prefers to use a member of their team who has knowledge of that particular business sector. This knowledge is often seen as far more important to the company than the softer attributes outlined above, even though the individual's personality may have a detrimental effect on the board. The choice of new directors then becomes problematic as it may have to compensate for deficiencies in the existing team.

Particularly in smaller organisations, cost considerations make it desirable to keep the board as small as practical, given the above constraints and the wish to have balance. Having fewer members makes it more difficult to get the breadth of skills that the board needs and more susceptible to being influenced by a strong individual. However, it can also be easier to build trust in a smaller team and to use this trust as a platform for more open dialogue but this approach only works if the new members are carefully selected for the qualities they bring to the board as a whole.

Decision & monitoring timescales

Each decision is valid for a given timescale: some are short term and some are long term. It is very important that the board is aware of the timescales for each decision it is making. Strategic decisions should have a long timeframe. Under normal circumstances, the organisation's strategy evolves relatively slowly and provides a stable background for developing the business. Operational decisions have shorter timescales but have a more immediate impact. The board must also ensure that it can track the progress of the implementation of its decisions. Monitoring takes place in shorter timescales which are linked to key milestones in the implementation process.

It is quite common for boards and executives to demonstrate their decisiveness by making too many changes, often to the organisation's structure, thereby risking destabilising the organisation and demoralising the workforce. The board must recognise that under certain circumstances any decision is better than no decision but, if this does occur, then the timescales for the decision's validity will be short.

Risk management

Risk management requires a combination of long-term planning and process implementation with short-term responses when potential risks are identified by the process. The board needs to be made aware, in a timely manner, of risks that have been identified as having the potential to damage the business and be satisfied that adequate processes are in place to ameliorate such risks. The economic crisis in 2008 further highlighted the criticality of risk management and the role of the board in understanding and challenging proposals for new activities, especially those such as securitisation which shift the timescales of the risks.

The critical element is that the board needs to ensure that it has the right information at the right time in order to fulfil its obligations. The onus is on each board member to ensure that they have the information for that decision and on the executive team to provide as much of this as is practical.

4. The roles of the directors

The make-up of the board

Before considering the make-up of the board (Figure 3), it is necessary to understand the primary reasons that each board member is in place:

The board needs to have an adequate spread of functional skills to be able to review the strategy of the organisation and the risks that it faces. There ought to be enough executives on the board, or available to present to the board, to ensure that key information on the organisation can be explained to the board by someone

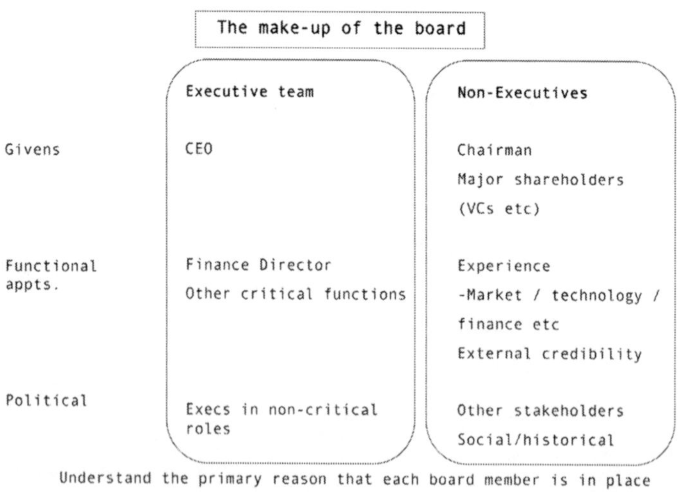

Figure 3

with the required understanding. It is recommended in guides to corporate governance that the non-executives should outnumber the executives.

The key executive directors are those representing the functions that are critical to the organisation. It is not uncommon for other executive directors to be appointed who represent non-critical functions. These are typically either political or status appointments. Such appointments should be used very sparingly as there are two very good alternatives that are available. The first option is to appoint the individual as an observer on the board, so he or she is able to participate fully in board discussions but not vote, although there is the risk of them being seen as a shadow director. The second option is to set up an executive committee that includes most or all board members and is used to exchange information prior to the board meeting proper.

Most boards have members who represent specific interests, which by definition are ‘power groups’ because they have sufficient influence to support a board member. Many companies that are young, small or both have the founder on the board. This individual may also be the managing director and majority shareholder, making it very difficult to have impartial board discussions. Shareholder representation is very important, by virtue of either having their own director on the board or having directors with specific responsibilities for investor relations. The lack of strong shareholder representation can be a problem for companies as it can significantly reduce the ability to succeed, particularly for specialist companies where the management team lacks commercial expertise or where the shareholders are likely to have to put more money into the business (Example 5).

Example 5

A small technology company had been developing, but not completing, an interesting material process for more than a decade. It had more than a dozen business angel investors, none of whom had a major shareholding, who had lost interest in the company thereby allowing the technologists to continue to play with their ideas. A well-backed entrepreneurial company with a related technology bought the original company. It injected some of its own technology and a lot of commercial drive. Within four years of completing the deal, the new company was publicly quoted with a market capital of several hundred million pounds.

In this instance, the original board had become too focused on their own expectations for a timely return on the original investment to see the bigger potential of the business. Effectively, there was a conflict of interest between their roles as directors and their position as shareholders and this strangled the business. This is one of the risks of angel investors. The company would have been far more effective had there been a time limit for each individual's tenure as a non-executive. It is also likely that the CEO was too focused on the technology and the original goals of the business to see its true potential.

Independent directors have a special role to play in companies where they can provide an impartial view to balance the potentially conflicting requirements of the executives and the non-independent directors since both represent significant power groups. Family-owned companies are particularly poor at recognizing the value of independent directors. It has been estimated that as few as 25% of family-owned companies in the UK have independent directors. Sadly, surveys have indicated that those that do not have independent directors also fail to recognise the value of having an agreed strategy for the company.

Balanced boards

A good board can make balanced, timely and impartial decisions about the current and future status of the organisation. In order to do this, the board itself must be balanced. The functional balance needs to reflect the nature of the business and its key drivers to ensure that the board is fully informed. The non-executives do not need to understand all of the main functional areas as long as they have the skill to ask the right questions, to assess the answers and to put them in the right context for the organisation.

The role of non-executives has changed from what was once a sinecure for the old boys' network to one having serious responsibility and accountability. The Higgs report (4) defines the role of non-executives for large British public companies and serves as a good model for other companies. A good balance is easier to achieve if there are fewer executives than non-executives on the board otherwise the power base of the former may be too strong to control.

If any director feels that they do not have a strong chance of influencing board decisions then either that individual is not suitable to be on the board or there is a serious problem with the way the board works. The non-executives should also control the nominations committee, if there is one, to make sure the right balance is maintained. If there is not then the chairman needs to take responsibility for ensuring that the board is balanced.

The roles that individuals play should also be balanced, as discussed in detail in Chapter 6. As an extreme example, if every director bar one took a quiet, co-operative role then the outcome would be very predictable. It is important to recognise that personal roles take on a different significance as circumstances change and the board needs to have a spread of roles to accommodate this, e.g. the strategic thinker would not be at his or her most useful when there has been an explosion at a processing plant.

Another important criterion is the balance of power. Investor representatives need to be very aware of this, especially if they are from a majority shareholder. They need to allow the executives clear space in which to operate and avoid the temptation to control the detail simply because they can. This is particularly relevant to shareholder representative directors who have a strong background in managing operations. Once again, the chairman has a critical role to play in achieving the right board balance and dynamics. If one person is both the chairman and the CEO then they wield so much power the board is inherently unbalanced. Whilst this is not recommended by the Combined Code, it is relatively common in the USA, reflecting another key difference in board styles across the Atlantic.

The key roles

The CEO

The CEO has a pivotal role in any organisation. He or she not only has full responsibility for, and provides leadership to, the executive team and the organisation but also is the key link between the board and the day-to-day organisation. The main functions of the CEO are, in order of significance:

- Developing and implementing the strategy, as agreed by the board
- Ensuring that the organisation delivers the performance that the board expects
- Providing clear and decisive leadership to the organisation
- Building and motivating a management team
- Ensuring that plans are being implemented – the 'chief progress chaser' role
- Ensuring that everything is in place to deliver against the plans – the 'sweeper' role.

In simple terms, the CEO needs to decide where the organisation needs to go, to lead it there and to make sure it arrives there in a suitable state.

In small and early stage businesses, the CEO will be heavily involved in all the listed functions as the management team is often too thinly spread to cover them. The size of such businesses does not preclude the presence of a highly experienced board, especially where there are external investors such as venture capitalists. Therefore, the expectations of the board regarding the CEO's performance are no less. The risk in such organisations is that the CEO gets buried in detail and fire-fighting and can lose sight of the bigger picture. It is the role of the board, and in particular the chairman, to ensure that the CEO retains the required perspective.

As organisations get progressively larger, the CEO should have a stronger management team and reporting structure to fulfil the lower level functions although the CEO retains full responsibility for them. The trade-off is between more functions with less breadth and fewer functions with greater breadth, reflecting the scope of the organisation itself. However, the CEO needs to retain direct responsibility for the strategic direction and for leadership. As others have put it, "a CEO is paid to think".

The difference in function and scope implies that a CEO who is good in a small organisation may be poor in a large one and vice versa. It becomes especially significant in rapidly growing organisations where the pace of change may outstrip the ability of the CEO to keep up. As CEOs need strong self-belief, it is not uncommon for them to fail to recognise such deficiencies in themselves. Strong control by the chairman and the board is required and sometimes harsh action is necessary to resolve the problem.

At the other end of the spectrum with very large companies, it is important to recognise that the best strategic thinkers may not be good at detailed implementation, in which case the CEO needs to be supported by a very capable Chief Operating Officer (COO). In such a case the CEO still needs to have a good understanding of the operational issues, the day-to-day implementation of them is simply being delegated to the COO who is his or her right hand man.

Leadership

There are two extremes in terms of style of leadership. Leaders may take the 'superhero' approach, being a charismatic figurehead who is very visible both outside and inside the organisation. Such leaders may become well known as they raise their own profile as well as that of their organisation. The risk can be that they become too powerful and autocratic and see themselves as being as important as the organisation. Interestingly, there is some evidence to suggest that leaders who adopt this style may actually perform worse than average.

The other extreme is to take a 'team captain' approach where the objective is to work with and through the management team and company structure. This type of leader can be self-effacing but this does not make him or her any less effective. The risk with this type of leader is less evident. However, there are times, particularly in a challenging situation, where strong and visible leadership can become critical to the effectiveness of the organisation.

Despite representing two extremes, these examples share the common principle that great leadership lies not in making people follow you but in making people want to follow you.

The board needs to be aware of the CEO's style and its impact on the organisation. It needs to ensure that the optimum balance of power is achieved in order to enable the CEO to deliver results on behalf of the organisation without encroaching on the overall power of the board.

A common characteristic of all good CEOs is that they build good executive management teams around them and motivate them by leadership at the personal level (Example 6). This type of leadership is based on interpersonal skills. Company leadership is based on strategic vision. Good CEOs combine both of these skills.

Example 6

The training report for a young army officer said "This lieutenant's troops will follow him anywhere – if only to see what he will do next". The lieutenant became the most famous British officer in the second world war, Field Marshal Montgomery.

The chairman

The role of chairman is very responsible and demanding. The emphasis is on communication, co-ordination and achieving the right balance. The core skill is decisiveness. It requires excellent interpersonal skills in addition to a sound understanding of the organisation's purpose. The chairman should develop open and direct relationships with each board member to ensure that their personal communication is effective within the board.

The key functions of the chairman are:

- managing the activities and operation of the board
- ensuring that corporate governance processes are in place
- defining a clear set of guidelines for board interaction and sticking to them
- ensuring that the board meets its obligations, both to the organisation and legally
- ensuring that the board is informed and makes balanced, sound and justifiable decisions
- co-ordinating the interface to investors
- being the primary liaison between the board and the executive team led by the CEO.

The chairman's role is very facilitative but it is essential for he or she to be a clear thinker and decision maker. In the event of disagreements on the board, the chairman needs to have the interpersonal skills to resolve the dispute in a swift, practical manner and the authority, where necessary, to take the casting vote whilst being confident that the board will accept the decision.

There are two main reasons why it is not sensible for one person to occupy both roles (Example 7): the role is very different from that of the CEO and the shared role undermines the constructive tension that a board needs in order to maximise its effectiveness. A joint role is far more likely to happen when the CEO adopts the 'super-hero' style mentioned above, making the risks of power concentration even greater. For the same reason, it does not make sense for CEOs to become the chairman of the same organisation when the CEO wishes to move on to a different level of work. It is unlikely that he or she would be able to make the required transition between two such distinct roles within the same environment.

Example 7

A multinational group had an executive chairman and a group CEO. The chairman saw his role as being strategic development leaving the CEO to run the operations and deliver results. In practice, these two titles were misnomers. The chairman was in fact behaving as a combined CEO and chairman. The group CEO was being forced to operate as a COO. This led to significant conflict between the two which only ended when the chairman left the group. Thereafter, the CEO was able to take full responsibility for his role and the new chairman allowed him scope to do this.

The chairman-CEO relationship

The relationship between the chairman and the CEO is the key axis on which the board-management interaction pivots as they are the lead representatives of the two teams: the board as a whole and the management team. Usually, it is also the axis between the leader of the non-executives and the leader of the executives.

The CEO reports to the board but for practical purposes he or she reports to the chairman. These two individuals should establish a relationship, based on openness and trust, between equals who have complementary responsibilities. The twist is that the chairman might have to fire the CEO. Their relationship ought to be strong enough for both parties to be able to discuss challenging issues and to decide how these issues should be presented to the board. If this is not achieved then the board itself will not work effectively.

In order to build a strong relationship, there needs to be regular contact between the two individuals, certainly more often than just at board meetings. If this contact does not happen, without good reason, then there may well be surprises for one or other of the parties, which is potentially damaging to both them and the organisation.

Developing the organisation

Monitoring

One of the primary functions of the board is to provide an arms-length, independent assessment of the operation of the organisation in order to identify risk areas – the monitor/evaluator function in Belbin (1) terms. The board and the non-executives have a duty to find out what is happening. They cannot simply wait to be told information about critical issues, or necessarily rely on what the executives tell them. Board members must be able to obtain this information for themselves from the organisation. In practice, it can be difficult for them to do this so there must be processes in place to enable them to achieve an effective level of monitoring.

The key risks often revolve around financial issues. The Turnbull report (9) addresses the issues of internal controls. A principal mechanism for addressing these issues is through the audit committee, where this exists. At least one of the non-executives ought to have sufficient financial know-how to be able to run such a committee effectively. The other main risk areas that the board needs to be aware of include markets, technology, production capacity, IT systems and especially health and safety, the last because the board may have greater personal liabilities in that area. All of these can be covered through adequate reporting and processes that detect abnormalities.

There is an underlying risk area in all organisations that is hard to monitor: rogue employees. These come in three main forms:

- those that exceed their limits of authority and often then try to hide it
- those that are stealing from or defrauding the company, or enabling others to do so
- those that want some form of revenge against the organisation.

Strong financial controls and warning systems should give reasonable protection against the first two although major organisations have been undermined by them. The third is more problematic for the board to protect against. However, the damage from this is unlikely to be serious unless the individual is a senior member of staff and such people are the least likely to risk damage to their reputations and careers by such actions.

Mentors and motivators

The board has a duty to deliver strong performance from the organisation. It has an implicit responsibility to ensure that the management team is delivering to the best of its ability and to change the team if it is unable to deliver a suitable level of performance. The chairman and non-executive directors should take the lead in mentoring and motivating the executive directors and ensure that the executive directors are doing the same for their management team.

The remuneration committee, which ought to comprise solely non-executive directors, takes care of the financial motivation of the senior management, although this is only one part of the process. The non-executives, under the leadership of the chairman, need to have processes to support and challenge the executives in a constructive manner in order to help them perform effectively. This is particularly important in early stage companies where the financial rewards can be both a long way off and uncertain. It is something that does not take place as often as it should in these organisations.

For mentoring to work effectively, the personal chemistry has to be right between the parties involved. This can be difficult to achieve at board level unless personal characteristics are taken into account in developing the board. Formal appraisals should take place for all board members and, if possible, need to be done by someone other than the individual's mentor. The key is that there should be no surprises at an appraisal – if they do happen then the support system has failed.

The appraisal process ought to be merely the formal output from an ongoing mentoring interaction between the individuals concerned. If it is difficult to achieve using internal resources then external coaches and mentors can provide support. This is particularly important for the CEO as it can be a lonely role from which it is easier to seek support from independent sources.

Appraisals are especially important for the non-executives because they provide a framework to discuss the board dynamics and to agree how the non-executives might adapt their roles to achieve the best outcome for the board as a whole. Note that it is far more difficult for the executives to change their roles on the board because of their other commitments to the company.

Strategy development & approval

The strategy should be the core road map for the organisation. It should have a timescale that is relevant to the organisation and be updated on a regular basis in response to significant changes in circumstances. The board is responsible for ensuring that the organisation has a sound strategy and that it is implemented effectively.

It is normal practice for the executives to develop the strategy with the assistance of non-executives as required. This is a practical solution because the executives will be much happier implementing a strategy of which they have personal ownership. The whole board then reviews, modifies as necessary and approves it. Most people who get to board level consider themselves to be strategic thinkers. If this is not the case then it can make the board's strategic review a very interesting and confrontational exercise. It is one of the occasions when the whole spread of skills on the board can come into play and where the board dynamics can be a major factor in dictating the outcome.

It is not uncommon in many organisations for the strategy to then be filed away and only dusted off for a quick look prior to the next strategic review. It can happen in corporate structures when people from the corporate office descend on a subsidiary to review their strategy. This annual ritual creates a strong tendency for the subsidiary to tell the corporate staff what they want to hear and then send them on their way. The main cause of this situation is when the whole group does not have a clear strategy that is used to guide the subsidiaries.

A key part of the solution is for the board to ensure that the corporate strategy is communicated effectively to the whole organisation. This allows each part of the organisation to demonstrate how its local strategy fits in with the larger one whilst expanding it to exploit opportunities within their own operating niche. Flexibility is important because a completely top-down strategy can miss important opportunities and risks, therefore, a bottom-up (or more strictly lower level-up) approach can make the whole strategy more robust. Another significant element is to ensure that there is a sensible balance between meeting the operational/tactical objectives and the strategic objectives. It is not uncommon for the latter to totally dominate the former. The operational view can be very useful in providing feedback to the strategy so it is important to be aware of the interaction of the two.

Once the feedback on the strategy has been gathered and incorporated, the final version of the strategy should be presented to the board and the key changes noted. The strategy then becomes a working document. The board must monitor performance against the strategy and ensure that the executive team is taking action to implement it whilst balancing it with the need to meet shorter term operational targets.

Information flow

A critical issue in the operation of the board is the level of information it requires to ensure the right decisions are made. The core approach should be for the board to be provided with information that is timely, accurate, sufficient and necessary to enable it to make a balanced decision. Clearly, the information has to be summarised to avoid burying the board in detail and the executive directors must take the lead in deciding what information to present. Controlling the level of information gives the executives considerable power. This power can only be balanced by the non-executives having access to any further information they feel is necessary and having the analytical skills to determine the right level of information. Giving the non-executives a thorough induction process and ensuring that they have reasonable contacts with senior managers gives a good defence against inadequate information flow.

It is critical that all board members have confidence in the content and depth of the information that they use to make decisions. If they are not comfortable that the organisation has the information required, for example because it is in an area that is unfamiliar, then the board ought to use external sources to obtain the information it requires. It is a far greater problem if some board members suspect that key information is being withheld from them by the executives. This undermines the trust and openness that need to exist in a board. Such issues need to be raised with the chairman for him or her to take the lead in resolving with minimum damage.

The executives will have a tendency, deliberately or otherwise, to provide only enough information for the board to come to the conclusion that the executives want (Example 8). In the event of problems, another tactic that executives may use is to provide too much information so the board 'cannot see the wood for the trees'. This can be a way of buying time for the executives to find a solution to the problem before the board spots it. The key issue that the board needs to decide is how much information is too little.

Example 8

The Finance Director (FD) of a medium-sized company noticed that the inventory numbers were rising at a much higher level than they expected. The FD was relatively inexperienced and adjusted the numbers to something more reasonable to have time to find out what was really happening. The FD told the board that the inventory rise was because an expensive new product was coming into production at the time and hence stocks needed to rise. After a few months, the apparent inventory level had risen by an amount equal to more than 10% of the annual turnover. It was only at that stage that the MD decided it was time to look in the stock room where it became clear that stock was at the normal levels. The company had to take a write-off of more than its annual profit and the FD was fired because the board had taken the information it was presented with at face value.

The FD had failed to make simple checks to validate the data and the rest of their board was too comfortable to check the information flow. The group's internal audit function had also failed to identify the inconsistencies in the numbers that were presented to them.

A key role of any board is to question and validate, to a reasonable degree, the information flow to them. Assuming that everything is okay is not a sustainable option.

Good information flow from the board to the organisation is also essential. The primary functions of management are to communicate, facilitate and lead. The board must ensure that the goals and strategy that it has agreed for the organisation are properly communicated to the executive team and through them to the whole organisation. It is also important that the organisation and its stakeholders, not just investors, are given the opportunity to express their views to board members.

Networks & contacts

In a growing business, the non-executives need to provide more than just a balanced view of the company. They are expected to have contacts that will enable the company to grow by using their network to access knowledge, markets, suppliers and money. In a larger organisation it is often the political contacts who are most significant because they have a proportionately greater impact on that scale of operation.

Venture capital and private equity companies often put a director on the board of their investee companies. Clearly this gives the investors insight and a high level of control but the upside for the company is that it gives them strong access to a source of further funding. Other non-executive directors may bring specific knowledge of key markets, production processes and other areas that are directly relevant to the company. This can become an important factor in the selection of a new non-executive.

The non-executives can act as an extension of the marketing and finance arms of the organisation. To be effective, they need to build good working relationships with their executive counterparts to allow an effective interchange of knowledge, which provides a good basis for them to learn more about the risks and challenges the organisation faces and thereby increase their effectiveness as board members. Any constructive relationship of this sort serves to improve board dynamics.

The same logic applies to the executive directors because they need to build strong networks with key customers and key elements of the supply chain. Raising the level of contact to board level is a significant statement about the relationship between organisations. It is an important commitment to partners who can then work with the confidence that the board member represents the whole of the organisation, moving the interaction towards a win-win basis.

Often the most important contact network that the board has is with sources of finance, both with current and potential investors and with banks. This network may be managed by a combination of the FD, the CEO and the chairman, depending on the level of finance that is involved. The breadth of experience and the contact network of the other NEDs can also be very important. They will normally have experience in similar types of organisation and, therefore, have contacts with financial institutions and individuals who are comfortable in funding operations in that market sector. The strength of these contacts often depends on the level of shared success that the NED and the investor had with previous organisations. NEDs with a track record of success can bring a lot more to a company than just their experience.

Conflicts of interest

Most people on boards have more than one role. In addition to their role as directors they may also have roles as executives or as representatives of shareholders. Any multiple roles raise the possibility of a conflict of interest.

The issue is specifically addressed in the UK Companies Act 2006, the implementation of which took place progressively up to October 2008, as follows: "A director of a company must avoid a situation in which he has, or can have, a direct or indirect interest that conflicts, or possibly may conflict, with the interests of the company. This applies in particular to the exploitation of any property, information or opportunity". The Act does provide that participation by a director with a conflict of interest can be authorised by the other directors but this should be the exception rather than the rule. Because this is a legal responsibility, any such director is open to much wider scrutiny and may be vulnerable if stakeholders from a variety of sources, including employees, customers and suppliers, choose to challenge him or her.

Executive versus director

Normally the interests of an executive director and the company are fully aligned but this is not always the case. The executive may have decided to leave the company or move to a different role and so might take action to maximise his or her short-term remuneration during that period by drawing forward profits to maximise his or her personal bonus. Another example is where an executive owns part of the intellectual property rights (IPR) that the company relies on.

It is the duty of the executive to make the board aware of potential conflicts of interest and the board can then decide whether to continue on that basis. In practice, most executives are good at working out how to get the best returns from their remuneration system and will have had plenty of time in which to maximise their own benefit well before they are in a position where they need to inform the board.

Director versus shareholder representation

In family firms and SMEs, it is common for the non-executive directors to be shareholders. Generally, in the early stages of a business, the shareholders and directors of such companies are a tightly-knit group. This bond reduces the likelihood of conflicts of interest, although family conflicts are not unknown. As the businesses mature then the shareholder base normally broadens, for example when transitions between generations of the family occur. When this happens, the bond between the stakeholders often weakens and, therefore, conflicts of interest become more common.

The conflict of interest issue is probably more significant when the director, often a non-executive, represents an external shareholder. It has been suggested that this element was included in the Act to control the actions of directors representing venture capital and private equity investors. The core problem for such directors, who are often partners of the investor organisation, arises when their duty to promote the success of the company is in conflict with their duty to promote the success of the investor's portfolio. It is the responsibility of the other directors to identify when such a conflict may arise and take action accordingly. Unless the board dynamics are good, these situations are recipes for conflict.

Director, executive and shareholder

The greatest potential for conflict of interest arises when someone is a director, an executive and a shareholder, as is often the case in companies run by owner-founders. Because the company is a separate legal entity, the owner-founder can be at risk by acting in his or her own interests at the expense of the company's, for example by taking funds out of the company for personal needs when the company would be best served by investing them. Once again, the other directors have a responsibility to recognise this issue and to take action before it damages the company. This is much easier said than done when the person who is being challenged holds all the power (Example 9).

Example 9

The General Manager of a family-owned business said: "Our owner-founder thinks there are two ways of doing things – his way and the wrong way".

Owner-founders have a tendency to be autocratic and to regard the company as their fiefdom, especially if they are the dominant shareholder. Their role as a board member ought to prevent them from behaving in this manner and make them recognise that the company is a legal entity with its own identity and existence. If they do not do this then the board cannot function properly. If this situation occurs then their fellow directors might be better off resigning from the board unless their real level of authority is brought into line with their level of responsibility.

Probably the greatest threat to such individuals is when their decisions are challenged by a stakeholder such as an employee. This is much more likely to occur if the owner-founder is autocratic but it is often not worth the complainant's time and effort unless a very serious issue has arisen.

Family companies

There is a further dimension to potential conflict of interest in family companies because the director may also be a family member. This is not only another role for the individual to play but also is one that has very strong ties. It can be very difficult if there is a conflict between the interests of the company and the interests of the family because the outcome could well be very damaging to one of them (Example 10).

Example 10

The son was appointed to take over from his father as chief executive of a successful family business despite his inexperience. He started a high risk venture which failed and lost a huge amount of money. The cash crisis that resulted threatened to bring the business down. The son then decided to sell a major asset owned by the business in order to keep it going. The asset was the multi-million pound house that his parents lived in. The parents had kept the house in the name of the business because it was tax efficient. The son chose to protect the business as a priority and put his parents out on the street.

This example shows the stark contrast between the attitude of the parents, who regarded the business as an extension of the family assets, and the son who saw the business as an independent entity. If this had not been a family business then the house would have been a private asset, not a business one, and it is very unlikely that the son would have been appointed as chief executive because of his inexperience. The parents paid a very heavy price for not keeping a clear distinction between the company and the family.

The situation is made more complicated because it can be very tax efficient to hold some assets that would normally be privately held within a business. For example, shares in the junior markets on the London Stock Exchange, AIM and PLUS, are free from inheritance tax. Currently in the Republic of Ireland, there is retirement relief which makes the first €750,000 free from capital gains tax for directors who have been with a business for over ten years and are over 55 years of age. This rule was designed to avoid having to split up farms when they were passed on to the next generation. Rules such as these are laudable and help to protect investment but they can lead to major conflicts of interest because they blur the boundaries between the business and family property.

5. Managing communication

Effective communication

Effectiveness

Communicating is something people have been doing all of their lives and, therefore, they assume that they do it well, especially if they have been reasonably successful. Often this is not the case, particularly when the individuals concerned are under pressure. A lot of research has gone into the subject with some very interesting results which suggest that there is significant room for improvement. Nevertheless, few people have had any training in communication. It is significant to note that most training initially emphasises the ability to listen. Only when this has been mastered does the focus switch to talking.

A key principle underpinning all communication is in understanding what the audience wants to hear (Example 11). The best communicators are very good listeners because this enables them to understand their audience and to assess how they are likely to react to any given communication. They also never underestimate their audience.

Example 11

During the preparation for a flotation, it was suggested that it would be helpful if the CEO had some presentation training. The reaction from the CEO was that he had been giving presentations all his professional life and that he was good at it.

The CEO reluctantly agreed to do the training course with his chairman as they were going to do the round of investor presentations together. In practice, the training was about structuring the presentation to have the maximum impact for a very specific type of audience in a short time slot. The flotation was successful and the CEO then acknowledged the value of the training course in achieving this.

In most communications that a board is involved with, the board members are in the enviable position of knowing their audience well so they should be able to communicate very effectively. Sadly, this is not always the case because on occasion they fail to appreciate the viewpoint of the audience.

A second key principle is to provide the right information at the right time, where 'right' is defined from the audience's viewpoint, not that of the speaker. All information can be considered to be time-stamped and to have a 'use by date'. This is especially important when using information for decision-making as it determines for how long the decision may be valid. Making the right decision at the right time is only the first step. Knowing when that decision needs to be reviewed can be just as important.

The board ought to have an agreed corporate communications strategy that embodies these principles and ensures that all stakeholders get timely information. The chairman needs to take the lead in ensuring that communication within the board is equally effective.

Interpretation

Relationships cannot exist without communication. The messages that are communicated, both intentionally and unintentionally, are critical factors in defining the interaction between individuals and groups. Virtually all communications are ambiguous to some extent and they rely on the recipient to interpret correctly what the sender intends. The nature of the interaction between people shapes the way that that they interpret their communications.

There is a strong tendency for listeners to hear what they want to hear – if listeners think the speaker is sensible then they put a sensible interpretation on the message whereas if they think the speaker is not sensible then they may put the opposite interpretation on exactly the same words. It can become a 'Catch 22' situation which requires careful and sustained effort to resolve. As discussed in the following chapter, it can become a critical issue on a board because of the strength of the characters involved.

Board members need to be aware that all communication can have a sting in the tail. If someone misinterprets the message then it will probably get back to the board one way or another. As most corporate communications ostensibly come from one board member, usually the CEO or chairman, there is a risk that the author of the message may be seen to be grabbing attention. These two factors combined can create friction on the board as a result of the CEO or chairman putting their heads above the parapet.

Purpose

Communication has two important and potentially conflicting purposes. The first purpose is to pass information to the audience. In this case, the objective is to provide accurate information at the right level. Too little information fails to achieve the desired outcome. Too much information can be counter-productive by confusing the audience or by diverting its attention from the key objectives.

The second purpose is to control the audience. The goal of this type of message is to get the audience to do what the speaker wants. Such messages are often 'economical with the truth' and may sometimes be deliberately misleading in order to deliver the required outcome. The risk with this type of message is that an intelligent audience will quickly realise that they are not receiving the right information and this undermines their relationship with the speaker.

Leaders have to make effective use of both types of message. However, their audience is in a very strong position to react if they are unhappy with the communication. Good leaders use a special form of the 'control message' in that it makes their audience want to do what they are being asked rather than doing it because they have to. This can only be done if the leader has established a strong basis of trust with his or her audience, whether it is a CEO talking to the board or the leader of a major public sector organisation talking to the public. Because leadership is a longer term relationship, the leader must be regarded as being honest by their subordinates if they are to maintain that trust. If they are believed to be 'economical with the truth' or, even worse, misleading, then their authority will be seriously damaged.

Scope

A board needs access to a huge amount of information about the organisation that it serves, ranging from the high level strategic plans through to detailed financial accounts, budgets and awareness of significant operational issues. In particular the board must be fully aware of the risks that the organisation faces. It, therefore, has access to a lot of confidential information. Knowing how much needs to be shared with people outside the board is a critical decision. Balancing the level and type of information to the scope of the audience is a major issue for all board members.

There is a crucial distinction between those within the organisation and those outside it in that all of the workforce will know something about what is happening and, at least in some respects, will know more details than the board. They should not be told anything that conflicts with what they know and the scope of communication must reflect this.

When communicating with employees and the outside world, the board needs to achieve the right balance between its duty of care to the organisation and its duty to stakeholders (Example 12). It is much easier to do this for good news than for bad. In challenging times, stakeholders want reassurance from the board. For very good reasons they want to know that their jobs are safe, that their investments are safe or that the products or service that the organisation provides will continue to be available. The board may try to protect the organisation by saying that proper action is being taken, plans are in place and everything will be okay. If they are too open about the risks then they can undermine the organisation. If they play down the risks then the stakeholders are vulnerable and the credibility of the board may be brought into question.

Example 12

An aggressive, consumer-oriented company had a dynamic CEO. He was a strong communicator who wanted to keep his employees fully informed. However, he was too open with them about the risks and challenges that the business faced. As a result, many became scared about their futures and their commitment to the business was reduced. Staff turnover increased and the business was damaged.

Such communication becomes particularly challenging for large public sector organisations where the public profile of the organisation can have a major impact on the perception of the board and its members. This in turn can affect the board dynamics as some of the board members may be more concerned about maintaining their own public profile rather than supporting key board members. When politics, either small-scale or large-scale, come into play then it can become even more difficult to communicate effectively, especially when it is in the interest of some people to undermine the communication in order to increase their power base or that of their political affiliation. Such politics undermine the ability of the board to work as a team.

Communication within the board

Communication versus conflict

A board should be a forum for open, constructive debate that leads to clear, appropriate, justifiable and timely decisions. Achieving the right balance of roles across the board is a necessary first step but this does not ensure the good communication that is essential for the board to make the right decisions.

People on boards are normally good at making themselves heard. However, as the key to communication is listening rather than speaking, the focus of board discussions should be to ensure that board members are listened to and understood before conclusions are drawn.

It is essential that the board is able to reach decisions. The more challenging the decision, the more likely that there will be strong differences of opinion across the board. Dialogue is essential for effective board operation but it is important that it does not reduce to a conflict or a clash of egos.

There are a number of key features that need to be in place to ensure that challenging discussions are 'constructive disagreements' which lead to making the right decisions rather than leading to conflict. The approach of the chairman is critical because he or she sets the tone for discussions. The chairman needs to:

- foster an atmosphere of open, constructive debate with good questioning and discussion
- ensure that all significant issues and views are raised
- identify the early warning signs of conflict and manage the discussions and individuals to ensure that the decision making process is not damaged
- cut short irrelevant topics to avoid distractions from the core issue, explaining the reasons in case they have missed something
- invite all members of the board to make an input to the discussion
- ensure that a balanced, sound and justifiable decision is reached.

These are very demanding tasks for the chairman but also make significant demands on the other board members. Ideally, the directors should have been chosen to cover the diversity of required roles but with complementary personalities. The latter is much harder to ensure than the former. It does not mean that everyone has to be balanced and calm because this can stifle creativity, although it does help towards having open discussions. It does mean that someone on the board must have the ability to draw the more challenging board members in properly to discussions without distancing other members of the board, in effect acting as a bridge to link them to the rest of the board.

In order to achieve such a difficult balance, the chairman must have a good understanding of the other board members' views, styles and 'hot buttons'. Some of the latter may be particular issues. Some may be fellow board members. An experienced chairman will identify and remember these factors. When the potential for contention arises, the chairman needs to be facilitative to ensure that the key players are allowed to express their opinions and that there is a fair interchange of views. If the difference of opinion does not resolve itself naturally as part of the discussions then the chairman must ensure that all board members have enough information to make up their own minds prior to a board vote.

On some occasions it will be clear from the board papers that there will be contentious points for discussion at the board meeting. In these cases it may be advisable for the chairman to discuss the issues with the directors who are likely to be most concerned about them well before the meeting. However, such discussions must not undermine the interchange at the board meeting, which could then be reduced to a rubber-stamping exercise without key risks being aired.

The most important task of the chairman, as the leader of the board, is to ensure that decisions are made. In order to do this, he or she must be a decisive individual. It can be very difficult for a chairman to be both facilitative and decisive during challenging board meetings, especially where some board members appear to take an intransigent position. The chairman's role as a facilitator does not mean that he or she is a referee. The roles as leader and decision maker must take precedence once reasonable attempts have been made to get a balanced discussion.

The board as a whole

Intra-board communication works at a number of levels including board papers, discussions at board meetings and interactions between board members outside the formal meetings. Within a board there should be no barriers and all members ought to have full access to whatever information they require. It is part of the board members' responsibility to obtain the right level of information to make a reasonable, balanced and justifiable decision without burying themselves in too much detail. This puts the onus on executive directors to ensure that appropriate information is available and to all directors, especially the non-executives.

Minutes of board meetings have an essential role to play. They must record the information presented to the board and the decisions it makes. They should also record enough of the discussions that took place so that the board can demonstrate that its processes are working effectively and that due account was taken of pertinent risks and opportunities. The minutes should enable the board to look back on and review how and why certain decisions were made because they may need to revisit them or the decisions have been challenged for some reason.

The main barriers to effective communication within a board are power-seeking and board dynamics. These will be discussed in detail in later chapters but there are some notable examples of the damage caused by communication failures within a board. Some interesting research (14) has shown that the average tenure of a CEO in the UK's National Health Service is two years and four months whereas it typically takes up to 18 months for them to settle into the role, even if they have undertaken a similar role elsewhere. The reasons for such a short tenure are often political issues within the board caused by a failure to establish good working relationships. This is clearly extremely inefficient for all concerned and is highly detrimental to the organisations.

The chairman-CEO relationship

This critical relationship in a board relies on open, effective communication and mutual trust. It is particularly important in public companies and public sector organisations as it is a high profile relationship which needs to be seen to be effective. In such situations the outside world will watch the level and quality of communication between the chairman and the CEO in external meetings and use it as an indicator of the strength of the relationship and hence of the board as a whole.

If anyone in the organisation is in a position to support and mentor the CEO, it is the chairman. It is very helpful if they can communicate at a level that enables such support to happen to some degree. It is also not good for the relationship to be too close because the chairman needs to assess the CEO's performance and be in a position to fire him or her, on behalf of the board, if the necessity arises.

The executive directors

The executive directors take primary responsibility for the day to day management of the organisation and there needs to be strong and frequent communication between them. However, their interaction and communication as a management team is quite distinct from their communication as a subset of the board.

As a group they are in a privileged position because between them they have direct and detailed knowledge of all aspects of the organisation. They are in a position to choose to share this with the rest of the board as they see fit. The way in which this knowledge is used is usually dictated by their leader, the CEO, who controls what goes into board papers and may also control what they say at board meetings and other discussions with non-executives.

Because the executive directors typically have specialist roles, it is easy for them not to pay as much attention as is appropriate to their colleagues' specialist areas. Their close working relationships as colleagues can conflict with the broader scope and objectivity of their roles as directors. The CEO should ensure that his or her team is fully aware of what is going on across the organisation and get them to talk to their colleagues if they are unclear or unhappy about what is going in those areas of the organisation. If this does not settle the matter then the CEO needs to be aware before it is raised at the board meeting and he or she should forewarn the chairman. It does not do the CEO any good if the board sees the executive team's views as being fragmented, although reasonable differences of opinion are to be expected.

If the other executive directors allow the CEO to control their communication with the board as a whole then they are in breach of their personal responsibilities as board members (Example 13). The decision they have to make is whether it is more important to acquiesce to the CEO's dictates and protect their jobs or to risk their jobs and hope the board would back them in a conflict with the CEO. This is not an easy decision to make.

Example 13

An authoritarian individual became the CEO of a technology company that had several major risk areas. The CEO refused to allow the other executive directors and the management team to discuss some key issues with the board. The executive directors let him have his way and the risks increased without the board being aware. The risks later materialised and the business went into administration.

The non-executives

In a well-balanced board, the non-executive directors are in the majority. Therefore, if they work together, as a sub-group of the board, they can wield a lot of power. It is important that as a group they maintain open communication and use this more than just in board meetings. They should share their concerns about the organisation and the executive team and ensure that they get the information required to satisfy themselves about the wellbeing of the organisation. The corollary is that the limited number of non-executives in general, and independent non-executives in particular, in SMEs increases the level of risk that such organisations face.

The non-executives have a key role to play on board committees, where they exist. The remuneration committee ought to comprise exclusively non-executive directors. The audit committee membership ought also to be predominantly non-executives. These committees provide a useful forum for the non-executives to build trust in their relationships and to communicate openly.

In practice, it is common for some of the non-executives to represent key stakeholders. This can mean that they see the other non-executives as competition because they represent potentially conflicting stakeholder interests. In some boards, the non-executives may also have political agendas which can have a major influence on the organisation. The chairman needs to maintain contact with the non-executives to identify when such differences of position may arise and to discuss them with the relevant board members to ensure that they do not impact on the overall effectiveness of the board. An exercise of this type can be very challenging in large diverse boards such as those of some public sector organisations.

Communication within the organisation

Talking heads

The choice of which individuals ought to take the lead in communications from the board to the rest of the organisation depends on the level of the message. For major events such as mergers and acquisitions, the communication typically comes from the chairman, using words that have been agreed by the board and its advisers. For normal information flow, communication between the board and the rest of the organisation is usually channelled through the executive directors. It is essential that the nominated individuals do so in their role as directors rather than managers because they will be seen to be speaking on behalf of the board.

People tend to be quite parochial, therefore, the board issues that are of interest to the audience get progressively fewer as the message moves to lower levels in the organisation. There are very few that are of interest to the organisation as a whole and, therefore, need to be communicated by the board. Getting the balance right can usually be left to the judgement of the executives and senior management but the final message requires approval by other board members.

It is important for all levels within the organisation to be aware of the board's role and how it impacts on them. It is also important not only for them to feel that the board is aware of that level's needs but also that they could approach the board, directly or indirectly. This issue should be covered as part of the employee's induction process rather than through unnecessary communications but it can also be reinforced regularly as part of the normal communication process.

The management team

The level of information issued by the board must always be tailored to reflect the awareness and focus of the audience. The CEO needs to keep the senior management team aware of what the board is thinking and the issues it faces as part of a regular communication process. Each executive director can talk in more detail with his or her direct reports to make the message more relevant to that specialisation. The senior management group is sufficiently aware and responsible to be able to deal with potentially difficult messages and it will need to be actively involved in action to overcome these challenges. Their level of authority should be respected by providing them with information but they must be made fully aware of what they can and cannot divulge to others.

The information flow becomes much easier if the board members have had contact with at least the senior management team, ideally having met the people involved during their induction process. This makes the board appear as an integral part of the organisation rather than as a distant body sitting on the organisational equivalent of Mount Olympus.

The 'awkward squad'

There can be serious issues in certain types of organisation where there are key people who may not buy into the role of the board. These organisations often have highly able people who are vital but who see their skills as more important to the success of the organisation than those of the administrative management team. This may be true and can happen, for example, in hospitals, high technology companies, universities and creative industries such as advertising. These senior people may see their high level of skills as being very transportable and which they deign to use for that organisation as long as the administrators do not get in their way. Their view of the board and the executives can be 'what can you do for me and why should I support you?'

The board and the executives need to put in a special effort to demonstrate to these challenging individuals the value that the board adds by offering them reasonable protection from external forces and giving them the scope to utilise their talents as effectively as possible. However, it must be made clear that the authority of the board remains paramount and that these individuals need to be seen to be working as part of a team, even though they are not normally team players.

Establishing the right level of interaction needs to be done as quickly as possible when new people are introduced, especially a CEO or chairman. Thereafter, the communication with this group of individuals needs careful attention to keep them involved without wasting what they see as their valuable time on trivia or wasting the board's time. Such individuals are likely to react strongly if they are not happy and they will probably express their concerns to someone on the board. As with all such feedback, it will have an impact on the way that some board members view others, especially the CEO, and so will affect the board dynamics.

The employees

Information that is passed from the board to all employees should be treated as though it is being made public. It is essential that the workforce is informed of anything that is going to be made public no later than when the public announcement is made and preferably earlier to give them the chance to consider it before someone from outside the organisation makes contact.

When all employees are told something that is not good news from the board or by a director, it is very easy for it to set off alarm bells in their minds. When developing such messages, the speaker needs to understand what the audience may have seen. For example, a production worker cannot be told that everything is going well, when they know that the throughput in the factory is low, unless they are given a very good reason for a short-term reduction in output.

Getting the scope of the message to be appropriate for all employees is very difficult. The level of information needs to follow the outline for communication by leaders, mentioned above. The initial questions that the speaker must consider are 'what does the audience want to hear and how should it make them react?' Once this is understood, the message can be tailored to achieve the objectives of the organisation whilst providing sufficient information to treat the audience with respect. Sometimes it may be better to split the message in two with a higher level message from the board and a more detailed and focused message from the relevant senior manager to help tailor it to the local audience.

Communication from the board can be included, where appropriate in the normal communication processes used by the organisation such as intranets or team briefings. Extraordinary communications from the board should be used with caution except for very good news.

Partner organisations

Most organisations have a range of partners, in the common rather than the legal sense, with whom they have very close links. Whilst advisers such as accountants, lawyers and public relations (PR) people are not actually part of the organisation, they are partners and should be treated as insiders with regard to communication. If there are any significant changes then their input may well be required so it is important that they are forewarned. The contractual agreements with these partners will include confidentiality clauses and so the board can, theoretically at least, be as open with them as circumstances dictate.

Key suppliers and major customers are in a different position but there is usually a significant degree of interdependency between the organisations. Where necessary to maintain their ongoing support and to maintain their confidence, they should be treated as trusted partners whilst being made fully aware of the sensitivity and confidentiality of information as appropriate.

Communication with the outside world

All organisations have a public profile, the scope of which varies hugely according to the type of organisation. Key contacts outside the organisation, other than partner organisations, include customers, suppliers, investors, the public and the media. The media is a means to an end rather than an end in itself but it is often the most powerful conduit to the public and to general investors.

Board members are seen as the leaders and the external faces of the organisation, normally with a focus on the chairman and CEO. Their formal contact with the outside world requires careful management in order to be effective. Such communication creates an opportunity to help develop the organisation. The individuals doing the communication also raise their own profile and they can come to be seen as the face of organisation rather than its servant. This is not necessarily a bad thing in the short term.

Certain types of CEO see their public profile as a career enhancing activity. They can end up promoting themselves more than the organisation, which can be damaging. Whoever conducts the external communication needs to recognise that they are taking on a personal risk. If the organisation performs well then all is good but if it does not then the high profile individuals becomes natural scapegoats and, therefore, vulnerable, whether or not they are responsible for the problems. Many CEOs have found this to their peril.

In terms of formal communication, the outside world only has the information that the organisation gives to it, either directly in the form of press releases and announcements or indirectly in terms of credit ratings, product reviews, approvals and the like. All of this is within, or an output from, the board's span of control. It is normal for only authorised individuals within an organisation to be allowed to make direct contact with the public and the media about major announcements from the board. The indirect information is a result of the organisation's operational performance which will affect the perception of the board and its members.

Formal communication only forms part of the way that the outside world views an organisation. Its role as an employer or as a supplier of products or services, especially those that are used by the public, can often have a much greater impact on that view. The corporate communication strategy needs to address all of these aspects in a coherent manner.

Investors

For public companies, most communication with investors is conducted through formal announcements, for example on the London Stock Exchange web site, through the Regulatory News Service, annual and interim reports and the AGM. This is good practice but is reinforced by the obligation to make the same information available to all shareholders, thus leading to interesting interchanges with the financial analysts and the investment press who are always looking for an advantage.

Major investors, especially institutional investors, expect to have direct contact with the chairman, CEO and FD and may want to contact them directly to discuss progress, often by having a round of private presentations when results are issued. Such discussions are critical in maintaining the company's profile and share price but they need to be carefully scripted and stage managed (Example 14).

Example 14

The FD of an AIM-listed company often had calls from small private investors asking about progress in the company and its products. These were friendly informal conversations. After such a conversation, one investor asked if he could share the information with a few friends. The FD agreed to this.

Two hours later, the company's financial PR advisers telephoned him to ask whom he had been talking to. It transpired that the investor concerned had posted details of the conversation on a bulletin board on the web for all to see and the PR company's alert systems had spotted them. Fortunately, the FD was very careful and had not said anything that he should not have done but it would have been very easy for him to release some information that was not theoretically available to all shareholders.

All investors receive annual and interim reports. The quality and level of information provided in these make a very important statement about how the company views its investor base. For companies with relatively illiquid stocks, the share price is often driven by small transactions between private investors as they often take a shorter term view of investments. The formal reports are a very important mechanism to express the business's confidence in itself and thereby build shareholder confidence. Particularly for early stage businesses, regular news flow is an important adjunct as it keeps the company at the forefront of the investor's minds.

Private companies are normally much more open with their investors because they are effectively insiders. The main investors in private companies, if they do not have a seat on the board, expect to have regular contact with the board and to have relatively free access to talk to the executives. Whilst there is not the same obligation to ensure that all shareholders have the same information, it is often the case that the main investors are from a closely-knit group who communicate regularly. If one hears something new then he or she will often discuss it with one of the other shareholders. The executives then risk irritating other main shareholders if they have not been given the same information.

The situation becomes more complex when a company is making a transition from private to public as all information given by insiders about the company needs to be validated. The opposite situation occurs when a public company is taken private. The normal due diligence process becomes severely constrained because the acquiring shareholder cannot be given information that is not available to all others. This puts the onus much more on the buyer than in a normal company sale process – a classic case of 'caveat emptor'. However, if as part of the due diligence process it transpires that the company has withheld significant information that should have been made available to shareholders, then it undermines the credibility of the board and the business.

The public

The public is in a special position because it can take on a wide range of roles including customer, investor and employee. Every individual involved in the company can switch between these roles, making the situation even more challenging. Effective management of communication with the public is crucial to many large organisations, whether it is conducted directly or through the media. If communication with the public is an important issue for any organisation then nominated staff should be trained for the role.

For many private sector companies, communication between the board and the public is quite limited but it can be very important factor in the public sector. It can become significant for businesses as part of their corporate social responsibility (CSR) effort. Smaller businesses often have a strong relationship with their local community and it is important for them to maintain this. Larger businesses usually take CSR very seriously for different reasons, not only for its own sake but also because their investors see it as an important indicator of the company's ethical basis and sustainability.

From a business viewpoint

The significance of the interface between the general public and a business depends largely on whether the public sees itself as an end user of the company's product offerings, i.e. are they business to business (B2B) or business to consumer (B2C)?

B2B companies normally have the lowest profile. They focus on their impact on the local community, especially as employers. However, if there are significant changes to the company's employment level then the board needs to manage their public profile carefully, both for damage limitation when jobs are lost and to make them seem attractive employers when they are recruiting.

B2C companies have a much higher profile because the public views the company through its product offering. It is more difficult for the company to control such views and brand management may be a key part of the corporate communications strategy.

From the public sector viewpoint

The general public has a particularly powerful role in the public sector because political forces, large and small, come into play and all public sector bodies are accountable, directly or indirectly, to the public. As a result, the boards of public sector organisations probably have the most difficult challenge in dealing with the outside world. They can expect the strongest feedback at board level from public disquiet about the organisation's performance. For example, the health and education services have very high political profiles such that even relatively minor issues that would not normally concern the board can become areas where board members have to speak to the public, the media and politicians.

The political constraints on the roles, finances and metrics of public sector organisations can mean that the board has to spend a lot of its time justifying its interpretation of government guidelines, both local and national, to its users and the public. This is a highly political situation that can put a large burden on the leaders of even small organisations such as head teachers of schools who may not have been trained to deal with the political fall-out of their decisions. This is probably a key factor in the relatively short tenure of some senior executives in the public sector.

Part 2 – Board dynamics:

People and their impact

Part 1 has discussed types of boards, how they operate and the roles that board members can play. Part 2 uses this view of board operation as a framework in which people interact. Boards provide a stimulating and challenging environment for their members. Despite the huge differences between organisations, there are certain common features that derive from a board's role and responsibilities. Part 2 introduces the Frame Model of board behaviour and uses this to examine how people and their interactions impact on board effectiveness.

6. Directors & their interaction

The two key features that every board needs in order to function effectively are a balanced and appropriate set of functional board roles and open communication which allows constructive disagreement. The roles that are functional at board level are different from those within the organisation itself. Boards demand exceptional people with distinct talents.

Achieving open communication is always problematic unless it is based on well established relationships. There are two reasons why it is more difficult on a board. Firstly, exceptional people have a propensity to believe that their view is correct. Secondly, the board needs a diverse set of skills. Therefore, its members probably have different backgrounds and approaches to their roles. The preferred approach is to use people who can match their strong functional ability with a broad approach. Such people are sometimes described as 'T-shaped'. They have an important role to play throughout an organisation but it is critical at board level. Their depth enables them to fulfil the key board roles and their breadth enables them to understand the issues being raised by the other board members. 'T-shaped' individuals are exceptional. Ideal board members have an open mind, a strong intellect, insight and relevant experience that they are happy to share.

The goal for the board is to harness these skills and qualities effectively.

Core roles

A view of board behaviour

The environments that boards have to operate in vary considerably, as discussed in detail in Part 1. However, there are certain common elements in the way boards work which derive from their core responsibilities. These elements can be used to develop a view of board behaviour and interactions. It can be difficult for board members to be objective about interactions in which they are directly involved. Problems can be made more visible and resolved by using a tool designed to help achieve the level of objectivity that the board and the organisation deserve. The Frame Model is such a tool and is described in detail below. It shows how a board interacts and highlights the significance of challenging interactions. The model can be considered either as a window onto board behaviour or as a mirror for board members, enabling them to stand back and look at what is happening within the board. This understanding can then be used to identify and resolve problems with board dynamics.

The Frame Model

Certain personality types are better suited to certain roles. A key part of the chairman's role is to define and manage the roles that each board member is required to adopt. This is normally self-evident for the executives but it needs to be carefully managed for the NEDs. In this respect, the chairman acts as the team coach to optimise the board dynamics and performance.

Practical experience at board level indicates that the core roles the board must provide are:

- Strategy - looking at the big picture – to be able to challenge and shape the future
- Operations – looking at the details – to make sure actions and plans are consistent with the strategy and will deliver the required performance
- Drive – the accelerator - to drive the organisation forward and overcome obstacles
- Monitoring risks – the brake – to be able to identify risk areas and issues and stop the organisation doing the wrong things.

Building a board to fulfil these complementary roles will ensure that the whole is capable of being greater than the sum of the parts. An effective board operates as an inter-dependent team when assessing opportunities and risks but as an independent team when making decisions. The latter is driven by the personal responsibilities taken on by each board member.

The four core roles reflect four separate and independent dimensions of board dynamics. The four roles form two opposing pairs in terms of interaction, strategy-operations and monitor-drive. These opposing pairs create a tension that underpins board behaviour. The result can be positive, if the tension is used constructively, but can also be negative and destructive. Board dynamics determine which of these alternatives will dominate.

Note that the balance of the two pairs does not mean that each role only addresses its opposite in terms of board discussions. All four roles need to be fully aware of the impact of the other three, it is how the personalities interact that turns the two sets into opposing pairs.

It is not uncommon for an individual to be good at both parts of an opposing pair. The four role model can be presented in a diagrammatic form (Figure 4), the Frame Model. It is particularly important to understand that it is a two-dimensional representation of a four dimensional view so the sectors do not show a continuum across the entire model.

Most people at board level will have strong skills in at least one of the roles although it would be extremely unusual for one person to be good at all four. Every board should have at least one, and preferably two, members who are very strong in each of these four categories, i.e. in the outer 'frame' zone. If a board member does not have real strength in at least one of these roles,

The Frame Model-core board roles

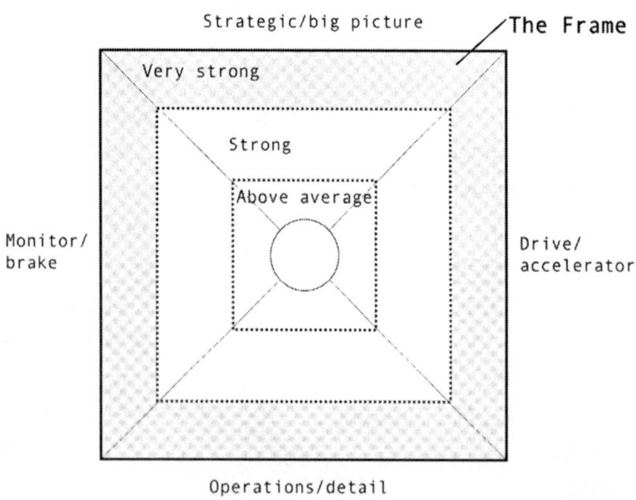

Figure 4

then there needs to be another very good reason why he or she is on the board. Note that 'average' and 'below average' do not even register on this scale as boards are the domain of the very able.

The required strength is relative to the needs and scope of the organisation: the board of a family-run corner shop does not need the same level of skills and strength as the board of a major supermarket chain. However, it is easy to underestimate the level of ability required by the board of a small organisation because it is still subject to major external influences. For example, the corner shop board would need much greater strength if the supermarket chain wanted to build a new site next door to it.

The Frame Model complements some well-developed psychometric assessment methods which are discussed in more detail later in this chapter. The monitor and drive sectors have strong parallels with some of the assessments in the Myers-Briggs Type Indicator (MBTI) psychometric test (15) which is widely used and highly respected. People at the extremes of the two sectors see and understand the same information but choose to focus on different aspects of it.

The strategic and operations sectors are more complex. These dimensions pose the greatest dilemma because people at the extremes of these sectors may see and interpret information very differently. Models developed by organisations such as Bioss (16) provide sophisticated tools to assess the breadth of vision that an individual has and how it develops during his or her career. Bioss has a seven layer model where higher levels indicate a broader scope of vision and understanding. Board level staff ought to have the ability to develop a meaningful long term strategic view and, therefore, should be in the higher levels of the Bioss model. People who only focus on the detail, i.e. at the lower Bioss levels, would probably be out of their depth on a board. However, the downfall of many an organisation has been triggered by lack of attention to detail. A board needs people who can understand the strategic impact of key details and vice versa. Such people are ideal to take on the operations role in the Frame Model. The challenge for a board is to bridge and encompass all of these views of the organisation.

A board requires people with sufficient breadth to provide skills in all four sectors and who can explain their ideas and views clearly to the whole board. Such bridging skills must provide effective communication paths to ensure that all sides of any argument can be understood by the majority of the board. Good communication is central to effective management processes. It can, therefore, be very valuable to a board to have someone who provides above average skills, but not necessarily great strength, in all four sectors because they can then act as a bridge between the other members. This is particularly important where the board has members who are specialists and are very strong but narrow. This central role is the natural position of a good chairman.

At first sight, the Frame Model may seem to court conflict by seeking board members with opposite approaches in the two key dimensions. However, as Alfred Sloan pointed out many years ago (17), constructive disagreement is necessary for the board to ensure that it has thought through all the issues. Effective communication is at the heart of constructive discussions and disagreements. Interpersonal issues and board dynamics can undermine communication and make a disagreement destructive.

Strong and weak boards

Examples of what a weak board and strong board look like within the framework of the model are given in Figures 5 and 6. Figure 5 shows a board which is weak because only two of the directors are strong enough in any of the four roles. It would be both unusual and risky to an organisation to have a board of this type. Note that this can arise even in a large board.

In contrast, Figure 6 shows a situation which meets the full requirement for a strong board. There are only

A weak board

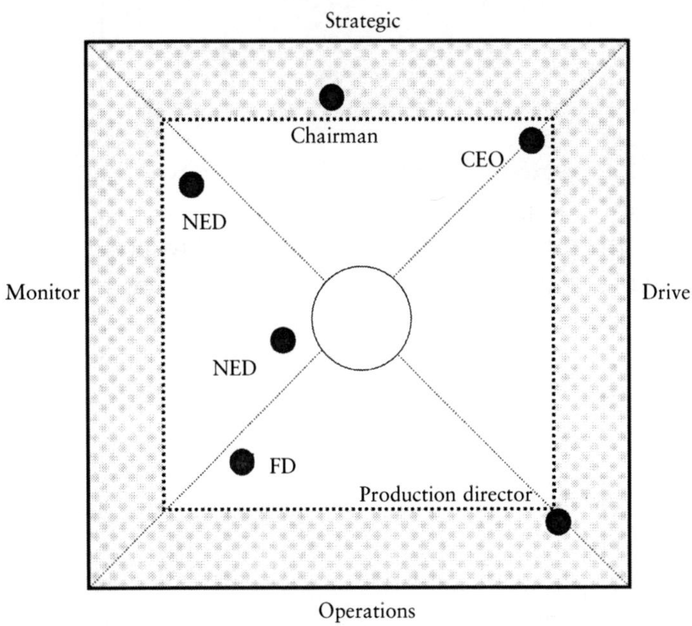

Figure 5

A strong board

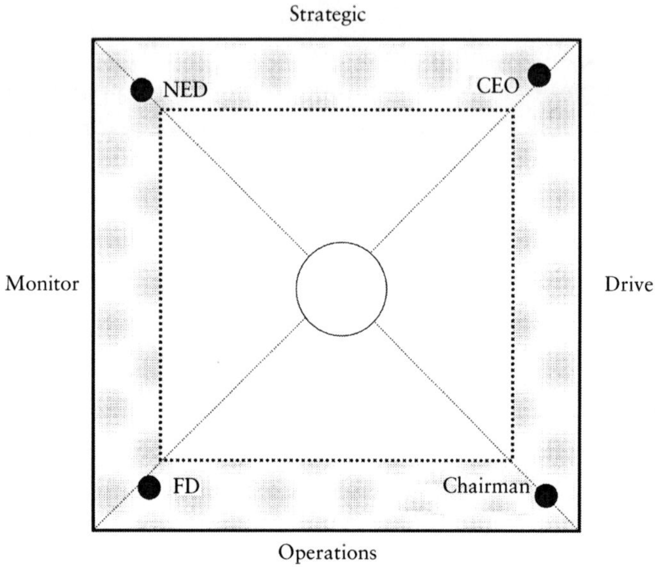

Figure 6

four board members but each is strong in two roles. For a board with this structure to work effectively, one board member, preferably the chairman, needs to provide an effective communication link between the other board members. Such a finely balanced team highlights the fact that, although individual board members are and must be independent, in this respect they are interdependent.

There is a general tendency for CEOs to lean towards the drive and strategic roles and for FDs to incline towards the monitor and operational roles, thereby providing a balanced team. If these two executive directors are complemented by two equally talented non-executives with the right styles, then a small board can be very balanced and effective.

A balance of opposites enables many subsidiary companies to work effectively with a board that for practical purposes comprises just two people, the MD and the FD, with occasional support from directors of the parent company acting as non-executives. There is a risk that such set-ups can also create problems because, in practice, many of the parent company directors may be former MDs whose personality is more likely to overlap with that of the incumbent MD than to complement it.

Role coverage

Because the strength required in each of the four roles depends on the nature of the organisation, the greater the scope and complexity of the organisation, the harder it is for an individual to fill more than one role. The complexity is loosely related to the size of the organisation, therefore, larger companies tend to have larger boards. The range of skills available in a larger team enables all the roles to be filled to the required standard as well as providing a breadth of experience to match the scope of the organisation.

For SMEs, it is reasonable to expect a good board member to have strength in two roles. It may also happen that one director has strength in three roles (possibly strategic, operational and one other) to a level that is adequate for a small business with relatively limited scope. Someone with that level of ability could probably operate comfortably on the board of a much more complex business.

An alternative view of the Frame Model

Within this chapter, the Frame Model concept has been used to look at the internal operation and balance of a board. However, the interaction between the same four roles on the board has a major impact on how the organisation as a whole behaves. The outward-looking view of the Frame Model is discussed in Chapter 9.

Personalities & roles

Multi-faceted personalities

People adapt their behaviour, consciously or subconsciously, to accommodate the situations they are in, the type of people they are interacting with and the objectives they are trying to achieve. They have multi-faceted personalities with each personality facet reflecting different situations. The concept of multi-faceted personalities is very powerful and is used to great effect in complex environments such as the workplace.

Most individuals have sufficient breadth of personality to be capable of adapting to a number of different roles. We learn as children how to do this in order to get what we want and the process then develops into something a lot more sophisticated in adult life. When individuals take on roles and responsibilities, they modify their behaviour to reflect those responsibilities and adopt specific personality facets appropriate to that particular role. It can be likened to a form of acting with a style adopted to achieve common goals. Any experienced manager will be aware of this and will do it naturally.

It is relatively simple to switch between personality facets such as 'work mode' and 'non-work mode' because the environments in which the two operate are easy to separate. It is much harder when different personality facets come into play in the same setting, as often happens on a board. Therefore, the likelihood of switching into the wrong facet becomes higher and the risk of making the wrong decision increases.

The role of director is very different from that of an executive manager. Therefore, the personality facet required for that role is also different, in a similar way to how behaving as a parent differs from behaving as an adult. If the individual is also a significant shareholder then that role again uses a different personality facet. Thus an individual director can have three roles to play on the board leading to four 'personality facets': their non-work persona, an executive, a director and a shareholder, thereby making the scope for error very large.

The individual board member should recognise that there has to be a clear distinction between the totality of their personality and the 'role personality facet' they need to play on the board because of the legal responsibilities they take on as part of a board. The different facets of the personality can create problems if the wrong one comes into play, thereby undermining the effectiveness of the board. Because the board has to make critical decisions, the consequences of such problems can be very dangerous to the organisation and also increase the personal risk to the individual.

Impact on board operation

People are asked to join a board because of what they are capable of contributing to it. The board must then be managed to ensure that its members deliver to their full potential. The personality facet that people adopt depends not only on how they choose to behave but also on their emotional reaction to situations. The former is very important because it can be adapted to achieve the best results for each role. The latter is more difficult and is often a reaction to challenging interpersonal interactions and environmental pressures, i.e. the board dynamics. Given the strength of the individuals concerned and the importance of the discussions that take place, these circumstances are very likely to occur within a board so board members may switch their behaviour and personality facet or even revert to another role. Any such changes are likely to alter board dynamics. They can also make the individuals concerned behave in a manner that is at odds with the reason they were invited to become board members.

The Frame Model provides a basis for reviewing the impact of personality types and interactions that can create problems within a board. Board dynamics drive the individual to a particular role or facet of their personality. Whilst a strong board may have been built, board dynamics usually drive individuals towards the weaker parts of the core roles and away from their strengths in the terms of the Frame Model.

It is important that board members are able to demonstrate strength in their core role when the board meeting so requires. It is also important to recognise that whilst a board may have all the requisite skills and roles, interpersonal interaction that pushes people towards operating in their weaker zones can neutralise not only their effectiveness but also that of the board.

If board dynamics work well, then the team can play to their natural strengths, thereby allowing all the directors to operate in the most effective parts for their roles. However, poor board dynamics can make a strong board ineffective. For example, if the chairman and the CEO do not work well together, they might fight for control. Each might undermine the other's ability to provide drive. Their battle can draw in the other directors and make them ineffective (Figure 7). The end result of such a scenario may be that the whole board becomes ineffective, despite the capability of the individuals concerned. If this occurs then the board changes from operating as 'the whole being greater than the sum of the parts' to 'the chain is as strong as its weakest link'.

Because the change in role is often an emotional and subconscious response, people can switch roles as conditions change or as different issues are addressed so it is possible for a board to change from being effective to being ineffective, and vice versa, several times during a

A strong board working badly

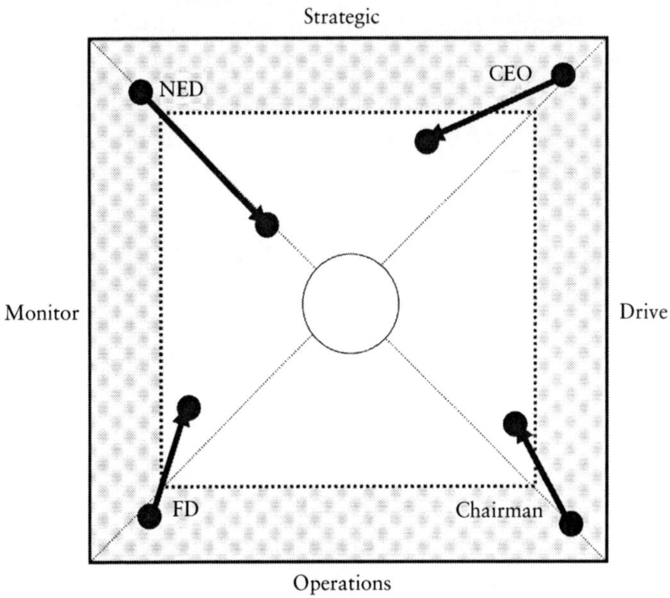

Figure 7

board meeting. Thus board dynamics can be dynamic in every sense of the word.

Board members typically have strong personalities. The Frame Model indicates that, rather than being a problem, strong personalities can actually make boards more effective because they provide sufficient strength in the four key areas. There is a risk that strong personalities can make weaker personalities less effective and thereby upset the balance but this can be overcome by good chairmanship and the careful selection of board members.

One implication of the multi-faceted nature of people's personalities is that it can take a long time to see some of the facets because the circumstances which trigger that facet have not arisen. It is difficult to measure the range of an individual's personality using psychometrics because these measure the personality facet that is operating at that time and even then it is usually the one that the individual chooses to show. As this makes it more complex to choose new board members, it is good practice to rely on the judgment of trusted individuals who have known the candidates long enough to understand the scope of their personality facets. The downside of this approach is that the board can become a clique. The chairman should be empowered to manage any issues that arise and to bring in new blood when necessary.

Assessing individuals

In order to work out where individuals fit in the Frame, it is useful to think in terms of simple metrics. For each of the four roles, the individual can be rated, normally by the chairman (Table 1).

Table 1

Score	Rating
1-2	Weak
3-4	Below average
5	Average
6	Above average
7-8	Strong
9-10	Very Strong

Boards require strong, capable people in order to succeed. An average rating falls a long way short of the required level and, therefore, only scores of above average and higher are considered of sufficient value to be plotted in the Frame Model diagram.

Most people's behaviour can cover a range of strength ratings, depending on circumstances, so it may take some time before the assessor becomes fully aware of each director's range. Note that it is common practice for people to assess themselves, and often others, according to the best they can achieve in any area, particularly in western cultures. This takes no account of the level which they actually work at in a particular circumstance such as in a board meeting.

Because the cost of getting the skill level wrong is high, the ratings ought to err on the side of caution until proved otherwise. This is especially important for new board members. They ought not to be appointed unless it is believed that they are very strong in at least one role. However, their assessment should start at a lower level and must not reflect this perceived strength until they have demonstrated it.

It is essential to remember that the ratings reflect the needs of the organisation. The same person could be excellent, with correspondingly high ratings, in a small private business but be poor, with correspondingly low ratings, in a much larger business, even in the same field.

Table 2

Director	**A**	**B**	**C**	**D**	**Number of strong ratings**
Strategy	4	5	10	9	2
Operations	5	8	5	7	2
Drive	3	10	9	6	2
Monitoring	9	3	6	9	2
No of strong scores	1	2	2	3	

Consider a board which relies on a number of strong ratings to make it effective (Table 2).

- Director A is quite narrow but could be a good sanity checker for the board
- Director B is extremely strong in drive but poor at monitoring and may require careful control
- Director C is nicely balanced as he or she is strong at strategy and drive and above average at monitoring
- Director D is unusually broad and may be capable of working successfully in an operation with greater scope.

A board comprising these four individuals could work well. It has two members who are strong in each of the four key factors and has the breadth to allow clear and consistent communication. However, the overall balance is only achieved because Director D has excellent breadth. If he or she moved on then, even though there is still strength in all four key areas, it would be advisable to replace him or her with someone with broad strengths. Small boards should not under-emphasise the importance of a linking role in order to provide good communication.

Note that with this type of assessment, it is possible for people to grow into roles so that they can show new strengths. An astute chairman will be aware of the strengths and weaknesses of the board. The Frame Model makes such changes explicit and, therefore, more amenable to management, particularly when board dynamics change the way in which people behave.

There is an added complexity in that people can take on different roles, depending on the subject in hand. Individuals tend to be more aggressive, i.e. in the strategy and drive roles, in areas that they are familiar with and more conservative in areas with which they are less familiar. Sadly, the latter does not make them strong in the monitor and operations roles. For example, the finance director might promote financial engineering options that others see as risky. The same finance director might take a very conservative view of a novel technology proposal. Such a shift in position does not necessarily reflect the real risk level but can highlight their lack of understanding and hence confidence in the proposal.

Personality types

In order to better understand the Frame Model, it may be useful to give examples of how it works in practice.

Whilst each board is unique, most board members and senior managers will recognise some distinctive types of personality that frequent the boardroom. In this section, several characters who commonly appear on boards are discussed and their impact on board dynamics is assessed using the Frame Model.

Dramatis personae

Boards are full of interesting and challenging characters. There are some personality types that can reduce the effectiveness of the board. It is often easier for people to understand and adapt to the behaviour of others if they can compare them to types of people that they have dealt with in the past. Attaching labels to different personality types can help in the process of dealing with them and in sharing views on their behaviour with others so this is what is done below.

Most board members have very valuable characteristics and add greatly to the operation of the board and its dynamics. The list below concentrates on aspects of characters who can have a negative impact on the board and who, therefore, need more careful handling to maintain board effectiveness. The character types have been given nicknames based on comments made by other directors and executives.

Autocrats/Control Freaks (who do not welcome board discussion because they think they know the answer). These types are usually the CEO but sometimes the chairman or lead investor. Autocrats seek to weaken the power of all other board members and to take this power themselves. This seriously undermines the monitor and operations roles.

Believers (especially in creative and/or technology companies). Believers often take the creative or drive roles and can be very good at these. However, their unswerving belief, usually in the business concept or the technology, undermines the monitor and operations roles. They can be very important in the early stages of a business but can become progressively more dangerous as the business matures.

Buddhas/benign forces (who think they are the fount of all wisdom. They will occasionally deign to share their wisdom with lesser mortals). Buddhas are frequently senior non-executives. They are usually highly able but are too aloof to allow their wisdom to be used effectively by the board because they want other people to ask for their opinion rather than contributing freely to board discussions.

Bullies (who like throwing their weight around). Bullies, as for bullies in all walks of life, are often very intelligent but may well be insecure. They challenge everyone, which is good, but they do it in a way that undermines people thereby threatening board coherence and decision making.

Cool Customers (the unflappable, rational ones). Cool Customers can be very helpful because all boards need people who are balanced and are good in a crisis. The risk is that they are so calm simply because they are not strong enough in any area to take the lead.

Crisis junkies (the board equivalent of adrenaline junkies). All boards need people who are good in a crisis but the 'I've seen it all before' style can just be a dangerous ego trip. By the time their skills are needed, it is too late to find out whether they are as good as they think they are.

Eeyores (who take delight in spotting things that might not work). They take the monitor role very seriously but focus on finding problems rather than finding solutions.

Grandfathers (who ensure that everyone's views are heard and that a balanced decision is made). Grandfathers are well-balanced and make ideal chairmen. The risk is that they may not be challenging enough and want to get to a happy decision rather than the right decision.

Judges (who focus on making decisions rather than understanding). Judges like to jump to conclusions and can stifle discussion. They overemphasise drive at the expense of the other three core roles. They are usually very experienced but their conclusions rely on their experience rather than board discussions.

Old Soldiers (who have seen it all before). Old Soldiers compare everything to their own experience and challenge anything that does not fit with it. They undermine the people occupying a strategic role. Unlike Judges, they do not jump to conclusions but can subvert discussions by attempting to limit them to their experience.

Paralysers (who will analyse something to death and focus on numbers rather than understanding). Paralysers can be a triumph of intelligence over common sense. They are typically younger, pushy directors who overemphasise the operations role and undermine the strategic role because it cannot be quantified in the way the Paralyser likes. They may also feel they have something to prove and have a running battle with the board's visionaries.

Pseudo-democrats (who welcome board discussions so that everyone else can agree with them).

Pseudo-democrats stimulate discussion and ensure a clear decision is made but want it made based on their opinion, thereby undermining the monitor role. Good chairs verge on being this type.

Show-offs (who ask difficult questions simply to show how clever they are, often associated with name-dropping). Show-offs are becoming less common on boards. They are often brought in because they claim to have either the ability or the connections to provide strategic options but in practice they are often just weak and should be removed.

Smiling Crocodiles (who agree when challenged face to face but disagree outside the meeting). Executives are very wary of NEDs who might be in this category. The risk with Smiling Crocodiles is that they undermine the authority of the board by trying to get board decisions taken outside the board meeting itself. They are dangerous and should also be removed.

Tiggers (who have boundless enthusiasm). Tiggers can energise a board and an organisation but they can take the drive role to an extreme and prioritise action over thinking. A Tigger is almost the opposite of an Eeyore and they can balance each other out or complement each other on a board.

Tornados (who are so strong and enthusiastic it stops others from trying and so get their own way). Tornados are usually very able, energetic and calculating. They are Autocrats masquerading as Tiggers because no-one else gets close enough to challenge them.

Usurpers (who think they ought to be running the company). Usurpers are often former CEOs who have become non-executives but are still used to being in control. They create a constant battle that actually prevents anyone from acting in the drive role. They may also work behind the scenes to get in someone they can control as CEO.

Weasels/Yes Men (people whose goal is a comfortable life). Weasels are often older non-executives whose goal is to ensure that they keep getting paid. Despite their ability, they go for the easy option thereby undermining the monitor role. This type is disappearing progressively as the personal responsibilities of board members increase.

Dealing with challenging characters

Because a board needs strong people, some of the challenging personality types outlined above can be constructive at the right time. Provided that they are managed correctly, such individuals may bring strong views and insights that can stimulate an open discussion on key issues. The downside is that they can inhibit other dimensions of the board and other skills that their colleagues have. Problems arise when they drive the board dynamics in such a way as to reduce the effectiveness of their colleagues and thereby weaken the board.

Such characteristics may be ingrained in people so it is possible that they will find it difficult to change their ways even when they are made fully aware of the problems they can cause. Because the characters are board members, they should be strong enough to face constructive criticism and accept others' views of their personality, although they probably will not agree with them.

Once the chairman has identified a problem, he or she needs to have a one-to-one discussion with the board member concerned, emphasising the value that he or she brings to board discussions but flagging the negative impact he or she can have. It must then be made clear what will be done to manage his or her behaviour and ensure that it does not impact on board effectiveness. In effect, the chairman needs to define a board equivalent of the 'Marquess of Queensbury rules' so that the whole board knows how the chair wants it to interact and what the core roles of each board member are.

Director's view & motivation

Why be a director?

In order to make a board effective, it is important to recognise how people are motivated in order to understand why they behave the way they do. For example, certain board members, such as owner-founders or the inventor of the business concept, will frequently not have a balanced view of the commercial strength of their idea. Within the non-executive group, representatives of investment funds such as venture capital or private equity managers may be motivated to balance the risks in their overall portfolio rather than to balance the risks in the individual company.

Most people's motivation combines a number of factors and so can be complex to understand. An individual's motivation, or the balance between his or her motivational factors, can evolve throughout a career as a board member. This is a subconscious development which happens slowly. If a major shift happens during their tenure on one board then either the organisation has evolved at a rate that happens to suit them or they have been on that board too long.

There are many different forms of motivation for directors to occupy a board position. These include:

- Status
- Title
- Success
- Reputation
- Power
- Respect
- Fear of failure
- Vision
- Money
- Comfort
- Making a difference
- Job satisfaction.

It is common for senior managers to see becoming a director as a major career goal and, therefore, the **status** and **title** of 'director' are their main motivations. **Status** is about how they see themselves. **Title** is about how others see them. The ambition which underlies both these forms of motivation drives such individuals to climb up the career ladder to bigger and better boards until it is satisfied. This ambition is a more focused version of being motivated by **success** and the impact on the board can be the same. Both **status** and **title** imply a willingness to take risks in order to achieve personal success.

Reputation as a motivation in business may be the result when people who have been motivated by status either reach their goal or recognise that they will not make further significant progress. In the public sector, it can be a much more powerful motivation as board membership can be seen to enhance an individual's position in the community. It is quite possible for people who are on boards in both the public and private sector to have different motivations in each, depending on where their primary career lies.

Power is not uncommon as a motivation but it is a dangerous one because it focuses on the process rather than the result. This is most common in small businesses and becomes rarer as the business gets bigger. It is less common in the public sector where power tends to be far more dispersed.

Respect for authority is common as a motivation on public sector boards and may reflect a wish to support other people's power and to be of service to the community.

Fear of failure is an interesting motivation. A fear of failure, including other people's failure, can lead people to take ever-increasing responsibility and eventually reach board level. This is not a bad form of motivation. It can be very useful but difficult to manage within a board, especially in organisations with an innate risk such as start-up businesses. The upside is that individuals who are motivated by fear of failure are likely to be very strong monitors, which can be the hardest role to fill on a board.

Many founders and creative people are motivated by their **vision** and want their idea to succeed. This can be effective in the short term because it enables them to overcome obstacles that would daunt other people. In the long term it usually becomes a significant problem to the board. It is not uncommon for the motivation of visionary founders to mutate as their 'baby' matures and often they become motivated by **success** as this embodies the effectiveness of their idea.

Money and **comfort** are not good motivations for being on a board. They usually reflect individuals who are reaching the end of their careers. If these are the motivations then the individuals concerned are likely to be 'yes men' and, therefore, ineffective board members. The pressures on board members mean that such motivations are becoming less common.

Making a difference is an important motivator in the public sector and in other socially-oriented enterprises such as the charitable and medical sectors. Visionaries and creative people often have this as a motivational factor because it reinforces their belief in the power of their ideas.

Last, but not least, **job satisfaction** is probably the best form of motivation at board level because it implies that the board member is driven by the scope of the work rather than its accoutrements. This is a particularly important motivation for non-executives who, because of the increasingly demanding legal and regulatory environment, should enjoy the intellectual challenge of the role.

Psychology of motivation

The psychology of motivation is a very complex area and many books and academic papers have been written about it. An important issue is that certain individuals are motivated towards concepts and others are motivated away from them. These are very different forms of motivation and, being opposites, they create a common source of conflict. Cultural differences can be a significant element behind this. There is evidence to suggest that Europeans are more likely to be motivated away from concepts, e.g. fear of failure, whereas Americans are more likely to be motivated towards concepts, e.g. the will to succeed.

Some motivations may be inherently damaging to a board. Differences between individuals' motivations can also create conflict (Example 15). These need to be understood and managed. It is important to be aware of the types of motivation so that, in the event that the symptom of repeated and destructive conflict occurs, the chairman and senior directors can recognise the cause. Motivation is usually deep-seated. The objective is then to make the offending board members aware of the potential cause so that they can monitor themselves. Although they may not be able to change their motivation they ought to be able to manage their behaviour.

Example 15

A VC backed technology start-up was run by a CEO with a good background in high technology. He was comfortable with the risks associated with early stage technology development. A psychometric test, undertaken by the VC as part of its due diligence, showed that fear of failure did not influence his decision making process, i.e. he was strongly motivated towards success.

In contrast, the staff joked about going on 'blame alert' when the director from the lead VC, who had a dominant shareholding, came to meetings as his focus was on identifying failure and allocating blame, i.e. he was strongly motivated away from failure.

Whilst the CEO and the VC director were on the same motivational axis, they were pulling in opposite directions and clashed frequently. The CEO left and the company stagnated. Both parties were quite extreme in their personalities so conflict between them was inevitable.

Better selection and awareness could have reduced the damage caused to the company by this conflict.

In early stage companies a strong drive towards success is usually far more important than fear of failure, hence the issues in the business after the CEO left. However, at later stages in the company's growth an excessive motivation to succeed could be equally damaging. Only broadly-balanced individuals can add value through the many phases of an organisation's development.

A sensible tactic is for the chairman to remind the individuals concerned, or make them aware, that their positions as directors are as distinct personality facets with responsibilities specifically to the organisation. Therefore, in effect, there may be a conflict between the individuals' basic personality, whose motivation got them onto the board, and the personality facet they need to use as a director. When their behaviour leads to conflict, making the parties involved recognise the different motivations that create unnecessary conflict usually provides at least short term relief for the problem. Longer term resolution requires a greater degree of self awareness which can be more challenging to achieve.

Psychometric tests

A small minority of people become board members and they do so mainly by exceptional performance. Therefore, board members are not 'normal' individuals. It has been noted earlier that they need to be able to take a strong role in one of the four core areas of the Frame Model in order to be effective. Their motivation can also have a significant impact on board dynamics.

Certain types of psychometric tests can be useful in reviewing these factors. As noted earlier, the Myers-Briggs MBTI test (15) can provide a useful input to assessments for the monitor and drive sectors. Specialist methods, such as the Bioss model, provide insight into the strategy and operations sectors. The psychometric test mentioned in Example 1 provided a powerful insight into a key issue that the company was facing. These types of tools are sophisticated and require professional interpretation.

There are also some simple tools that are freely available, at least in their basic forms, which can be used without professional assistance to provide useful insights into behaviour. These include:

- Belbin team role analysis (1) - for team roles
- Learning Styles (18) – to assess how individuals approach problems.

These tools are not to be treated as tests that new board members must pass to be accepted. The results of psychometric tests are not fixed as they may alter depending on the individual's circumstances at a point in time. In many respects, the primary goal of getting people to undertake such tests is to make them think about their own make-up and behaviour and about how this then impacts on those around them. They are also there to help the chairman, the Human Resources (HR) Director and the board understand how the members can work together as a team in the most effective manner.

It is important to recognise that board members often fall into particular psychometric types because of the nature of their work. For example, directors from investors such as venture capital, private equity or banks may well have a similar approach. In addition, they will have a personality facet which is driven by their primary role as an investor. A similar situation can arise with boards of family firms because the family members that work in the business may choose to do so because they fit a shared personality type. This common style can skew the balance of the board and the external directors need to recognise the impact it may have on board dynamics.

Belbin team types on the board

The Belbin analysis (1) is probably the best known method for looking at team interactions. It uses a simple analysis, which was empirically derived, and describes the types of roles that people play in a team. The assessment quantifies how much each individual tends to play each type of role. People are primarily categorised by the types in which they have the strongest preferences, even though the distribution can range from polarised to very broad. This mix of preferences is very important in making a team work effectively.

The Belbin analysis provides a useful way of looking at boards and, indeed, any team. Once team members understand the role that they are inclined to play in a given team, it also helps them to interact with the team more effectively or even to work in a different role in which they are relatively strong. Not all roles have the same significance at board level because some can be filled by senior management roles.

Particularly relevant Belbin types:

The roles that are very important at board level are the Shaper, Co-ordinator and Monitor/Evaluator (Figure 8).

These are often supported by Completer/Finishers and Specialists. The core attributes of these team roles are shown in Table 3.

Table 3

Team role	Contribution	Allowable weakness
Shaper	Challenging, dynamic, thrives on pressure. The drive and courage to overcome obstacles.	Prone to provocation. Offends people's feelings.
Co-ordinator	Mature, confident, a good chair. Clarifies goals, promotes decision-making, delegates well.	Can be seen as manipulative. Offloads personal work.
Monitor/ Evaluator	Sober, strategic and discerning. Sees all options. Judges accurately.	Lacks drive and ability to inspire others.
Completer/ Finisher	Painstaking, conscientious, anxious. Searches out errors and omissions. Delivers on time.	Inclined to worry unduly. Reluctant to delegate.
Plant	A creative problem solver	Can be a poor communicator
Specialist	Single-minded, self-starting, dedicated. Provides knowledge and skills in rare supply.	Contributes only on a narrow front. Dwells on technicalities.

Ideally the CEO has **Shaper** preferences but Sales Directors and non-executive directors often come into this category.

It is very helpful if the chairman has a **Co-ordinator** preference as it is a perfect fit. The weakness concerning personal work is not relevant to a non-executive director.

Finance Directors usually have **Monitor/Evaluator** preferences although this may not be their strongest type. It is normal for some non-executive directors to share these traits.

Elements of the **Completer/Finisher** preference are a useful additional role at board level as they bring a focus on delivery. If this role is taken, it is normally by Production Directors. However, a good Chairman can obviate the need for this role.

The **Plant** is very helpful in developing strategies. This role is important in organisations which are growing or facing new challenges. Because they can be poor communicators, they make bad chairman.

Technical Directors and Creative Directors probably have **Specialist** preferences and they are frequently the people whose idea is behind the business. Owner-founders often migrate into these roles as the company matures.

Note that Belbin analysis is about preference types so people can choose, deliberately or unwittingly, to exhibit certain types and preferences in specific team situations. Most people have tendencies to more than one role and, therefore, it is easy for the balance to shift as circumstances change. Any members of the team can flex their style if necessary, at least in theory.

A theoretical mapping of Belbin types onto the four core areas of the Frame Model gives the **Shaper** for Drive, the **Co-ordinator** for Strategy, the **Monitor-Evaluator** for Monitor and the **Completer-Finisher** for Operations.

The Belbin analysis has two other types which are less relevant on a board but are included here for the sake of completeness. The **Resource Investigator** gives a team a good start to a project by vigorously pursuing contacts and opportunities. He or she is focused outside the team and has a finger on the pulse of the outside world. A **Resource Investigator** can lose momentum towards the end of a project and forget small details. A **TeamWorker** is the oil between the cogs that keeps the team running. Because of an unwillingness to take sides, a **TeamWorker** may not be able to take decisive action when it is needed.

Belbin team types on the board

Executives
Normally contribute:
- Shaper (often the CEO)
- Implementer
- Specialists
- Completer/Finishers

Can give extra support
- Co-ordinator (also a good CEO)
- Monitor/Evaluator

Non-executives
Normally contribute:
- Co-ordinator (usually the Chairman)
- Monitor/Evaluator

Can give extra support
- Shaper

The roles of Resource Investigator and Plant could be filled by either executive or non-executive personnel

Figure 8

Learning styles

Learning styles are a way of looking at how people prefer to behave and hence address problems. There are many different versions of the learning styles model with subtle differences. One of the simplest models to understand was developed by David Kolb (18). Kolb categorises people in four ways; activist, pragmatist, theorist and reflector. The differences between the four categories can be illustrated by how they would learn to ride a bike:

- the activist would get on the bike and try to ride it
- the pragmatist would watch someone else ride it and then try
- the theorist would look at the principles behind riding a bike
- the reflector would think about why they might want to ride a bike.

A balanced team has a mix of all four types but the **pragmatist** and the **theorist** are probably the most important for a board. The **activist** is important for executive management roles provided the board has assessed the risks and agreed what must be done. The **reflector** may slow down decision-making in any group but it is always useful to have someone who stands back and asks the question 'why?' **Reflectors** can be very good at strategy because of the effort to think round problems. It then leaves an interesting challenge for the chairman to get them to share their thought processes with the rest of the board.

Learning styles are a very important aspect of team structure because people normally prefer working with others who have a similar learning style (Example 16). In particular there may be conflict between activists and reflectors that can be very damaging.

Example 16

A long established family business was having problems in making a key strategic decision and sought external advice. The board comprised the family shareholders, most of whom also had executive roles, and a managing director and non-executive chairman who were both from outside the family. The previous MD had been removed a couple of years previously because his style did not fit. Probably he was the type or person they needed in order to shake up their thinking but the shareholders did not want to be challenged in this way. The business had done reasonably well in good market conditions but was struggling to cope with a more challenging business environment.

The advisors recognised that the core problem was not the strategic issue but the way in which the board operated. They asked the board members, who were initially reluctant, to undergo Belbin analysis and learning styles assessments. The Belbin review showed that the group lacked a number of key roles, including monitor/evaluator and plant, which meant that they could close too quickly on ideas without systematically looking for others and they lacked the natural ability to critically evaluate any decision they did make. The learning styles review showed that they were predominantly theorists and reflectors; their approach was to discuss at length a limited number of options (due to the lack of plants) and taking action was difficult.

Given the predominance of family members on the board, their family traits made them prefer to work with like-minded people. The assessment helped the board members to become aware of their own styles and preferences and hence helped them to make a more balanced decision. The risk was that the board members would simply revert to type when the advisors left.

The large majority of family businesses do not have independent directors. This example highlights some of the risks associated with the board not being a balanced team. Good independent non-executive directors are the primary tool a board has to overcome such limitations.

There is a good match between learning styles and the personality types mentioned earlier. For example:

- the Tornado is usually an activist
- the Believer is usually a theorist and
- the Cool Customer is usually a pragmatist.

Executive versus non-executive styles

The interactions of executive and non-executive directors with an organisation are very different. Therefore, it is reasonable to expect their interaction with the board to be very different. It is part of the role of non-executive directors to provide breadth of knowledge and contacts. They also have a responsibility to monitor, and occasionally mentor, executives. This gives them both a 'gamekeeper' and a 'poacher' role. The key is for them to be able to challenge the executives in a constructive and non-confrontational manner.

Executive directors must know the organisation intimately and have a good grasp of the detail. This depth of knowledge should be complemented by the breadth of the non-executives. It is not uncommon for the executive team's closeness to the organisation to make them reject the 'outside' knowledge, comments and criticism of the rest of the board.

From the executives' viewpoint there can be two very different types of non-executive: ones that do not represent a power base and those that do. Non-executives who represent a major stakeholder, particularly ones with a controlling interest or who are key sources of funding, may see their role as being to control the executives rather than support them. Even if it is just the way that the executives view them, it upsets the balance of power and can easily lead to conflict. Such NEDs are far less likely to be accepted as advisers or mentors by the executives. Non-executives who do not represent a power base are far less threatening and can be much easier for the executives to interact with. This openness is why independent directors are so important, especially on SMEs, including those that are family-owned or venture capital backed.

In order for the board to exercise its collective responsibility, board members need to co-operate in sharing information, reviewing it and deciding the way forward. Good boards have no fear of sharing information and no fear of being challenged. Occasional confrontation may arise simply because of the diversity of personalities and styles across the board. This should be contained and it is essential that any such confrontation does not create resentment. Failing to challenge the board is also a risk. Therefore, the chairman and the board members have to achieve a difficult balance by stimulating a good, open and constructive debate and reaching a consensus view.

There is an easy but flawed status quo, especially in the eyes of some executive directors, which sets the non-executive directors as the inquisitors and the executives as the accused. Non-executives often consider themselves to be providing helpful advice to the executives which the executives regard as interference. It is the responsibility of the chairman to set the tone of board discussions at the right level, to act quickly to resolve clashes and to reinforce a sense of collective responsibility that binds the board together.

The core issue is how each individual affects their fellow board members. Someone with poor interpersonal skills brings others down to their level. Someone with good interpersonal skills may increase the strength of others. Harnessing this positive influence is the key to the effective use of board dynamics. The balance between executives, independent non-executives and tied non-executives also has a major impact. These factors set the underlying framework for board dynamics. A balanced board structure is much easier to achieve from the outset than to balance the personalities on the board. Therefore, this must be a priority when building boards.

Problems can be minimised by building better relationships between the non-executives and the executive directors. In particular the relationship should not be confined to board meetings. A good induction programme for new directors may be used to provide a thorough grounding in the operation of the organisation and to enable the new board member to get to know his or her fellow directors well. These relationships can be reinforced by off-site board meetings which include social interaction. The goal is for all directors to feel comfortable about having a 'how is it going?' chat with any of their colleagues without undermining their ability to challenge them, very strongly if necessary, when the need arises.

'Glass ceilings'

A sensible way of ensuring that the board's operations are open and balanced is to get a good spread of types of people as well as types of personalities. The conservative culture of the boardroom may try to counter this by erecting 'glass ceilings' to keep out the 'wrong sort' of people.

Most organisations that put up glass ceilings are not fully aware that this is what they are doing. In their view, they are simply picking new people for the role who have the right approach and understanding. The new people can all too easily be clones of the existing board members. As with all forms of discrimination, it may require positive action by external groups to initiate change. Any reasonable board will welcome the breadth of views that diversity can bring. This breadth can often better reflect the nature of the organisation's marketplace whilst increasing the likelihood of building a strong board based on the four core roles of the Frame Model. It is interesting to note that because of the strong external pressures on public sector boards, they often have a much more diverse membership than private sector boards.

Two particular examples of glass ceilings are discussed below.

Women on boards

In the UK, women hold a remarkably low percentage of board positions and some surveys have indicated that it may be falling. At the moment only 2% of CEOs of the companies listed on London's AIM market are women. In contrast, studies into the effectiveness of women on boards indicate that boards which include women make better balanced decisions than all male boards. Other studies have indicated that women are more successful at growing revenues and much better at using capital than their male counterparts in venture-backed European companies (19). Therefore, evidence indicates that women on a board can add significantly to its effectiveness.

Because women generally take a broader view, an understanding of board dynamics suggests that a mixed gender board will operate very differently from an all male board. It has the potential to be better balanced and, thus, more effective. Not having more women on boards is far more than a waste of talent, it is also a wasted opportunity.

There are a few positive indications that the deficiency is starting to be rectified, with some surveys suggesting that 20% of recent appointments to FTSE 100 companies are female. This growth suggests that large companies have recognised the opportunity that a mixed gender board offers but there is still a significant imbalance on the huge majority of boards.

Nationality

There are other forms of glass ceiling that can arise because of nationality, rather than the cultural issues that are discussed in the next chapter. It is particularly relevant in multinational companies where an understanding of the different cultures is important. Nevertheless, such boards are typically dominated by people from the organisation's home country. The reasons given for excluding foreigners from the board include not understanding the local investor culture, national security and other creative forms of barrier (Example 17). Such obstacles are more likely to be used in countries that see themselves as more distinct from the international business norm, either because of language, culture or both. It is less likely to apply, for example, with Americans directors on British boards or vice versa, Sarbanes-Oxley (7) permitting.

Example 17

A very able Irishman worked in the home country of a major European multinational group and rose rapidly to become Director of Marketing for the subsidiary which covered the group's home territory. He had a very good working relationship with his boss who was on the main board. One day the boss called him in and as a favour told him that despite all his good work, he would never become a main board director because he was a foreigner.

The company did a lot of work in the defence sector and the board felt they needed nationals on the board to maintain their position in the domestic defence market, despite the fact that the majority of their defence business was export. Of course, none of this was written down and the Irishman left to found a successful company of his own.

The unusual thing about this example is that the individual was actually told of the situation. This saved him a lot of time in building his subsequent, successful career. Normally such things are implicit and unspoken and the victims are left to draw their own conclusions.

7. The cultural dimension

It is becoming increasingly recognised that diversity can benefit a board. The Tyson report (11) emphasises the benefits of bringing a broader range of people onto boards. For boards of multinational companies, or those for whom export is a major part of their business, it is very important to understand different cultures (Example 18). For example, it is particularly important for contractual negotiations where Western culture is very different from that in the Middle East or Asia.

Example 18

A multinational European business had run operations successfully across Europe and the Americas. The economic growth in Asia made it an attractive market and the company decided to set up subsidiaries to win major contracts in the region. The new operations were run by expatriates who were successful initially in winning large orders. However, serious problems arose in trying to fulfil these contracts.

The CEO was 'culturally challenged' and was unwilling to try to understand the cultural differences. He put the blame for most of the problems in the new operations on the different business culture which he described in highly derogatory terms. After the belated introduction of managers who were sensitive to the cultural issues, most of the work was completed and a significant proportion of the payments were received. Following a change in strategy by the board, the Asian operations were then closed down, losing 'face' and making it very difficult for the company to re-enter this potentially lucrative market in the future.

Many Asian countries, particularly those in East Asia, take a longer-term view of business and of relationships. In setting up its operations in Asia, this company had made short-term decisions based on the opportunities it had seen. It had failed to understand the cultures and the business climate it was moving into. This lack of cultural planning undermined its expansion strategy and damaged the business in the long-term.

It has been suggested that globalisation can only succeed at a superficial level because of deep-seated cultural differences. The dictum 'think global, act local' is a very sensible approach to apply in order to overcome the issues that arise, although it can prove difficult to achieve in practice.

When people from different nationalities and cultures sit on the same board, it can have a significant effect in two ways. Firstly, there may be important differences in the legal and regulatory environments between countries. It is possible that an overseas board member may have a different understanding and approach to the mechanics of board operation. This is something that can be taken care of as part of the induction process. Secondly, the different personal and cultural background can have a major impact on board dynamics. This situation is difficult to manage because it derives from ingrained rather than learned behaviour. Cultural differences need to be fully appreciated and accommodated if a multicultural board is to work effectively. All multinational organisations need to embrace and exploit cultural differences and they should be reflected in the composition of the board.

Culture differences

A large body of work has gone into understanding and analysing cultural differences. It is an extremely complex subject and some excellent work has been undertaken in this area. Amongst the best known examples are those developed by Fons Trompenaars and Geert Hofstede. Both of these sources provide an insightful, detailed but complex analysis. Trompenaars' work focuses on the business implications of culture whilst Hofstede takes a broader social view. A brief summary of their work is given below. Interested parties can use the original references for more information on the two models. A search of the web will reveal more on the broad range of work undertaken in this area by these two leading researchers.

Trompenaars' culture difference factors

Fons Trompenaars (20) was one of the first to show professional managers how to build the cross-cultural skills, sensitivity and awareness required in a global business environment. He recognised that every culture distinguishes itself from others by the specific solutions it chooses to problems which reveal themselves as 'dilemmas'. Trompenaars looks at these problems under three headings: those which arise from relationships with other people, those which arise from the passage of time and those which relate to the environment.

The first of these, which concerns relationships with other people, gives rise to five culture dimensions:

- Universalism versus particularism = rules versus relationships
- Individualism versus communitarianism = the group versus the individual
- Neutral versus emotional = the range of feelings expressed
- Specific versus diffuse = the range of involvement
- Achievement versus ascription = how status is accorded.

Three aspects of organisational structure are especially important in determining corporate culture:

- The general relationship between employees and their organisation
- The vertical or hierarchical system of authority defining superiors and subordinates
- The general views of employees about the organisation's destiny, purpose, goals and their places in this.

The dimensions Trompenaars used to distinguish corporate culture are 'equality-hierarchy' and 'orientation to the person - orientation to the task'. Overall, this enables the definition of four types of corporate culture which vary significantly in how they think and form teams. Trompenaars thus creates four metaphors for culture: family, Eiffel Tower, guided missile and

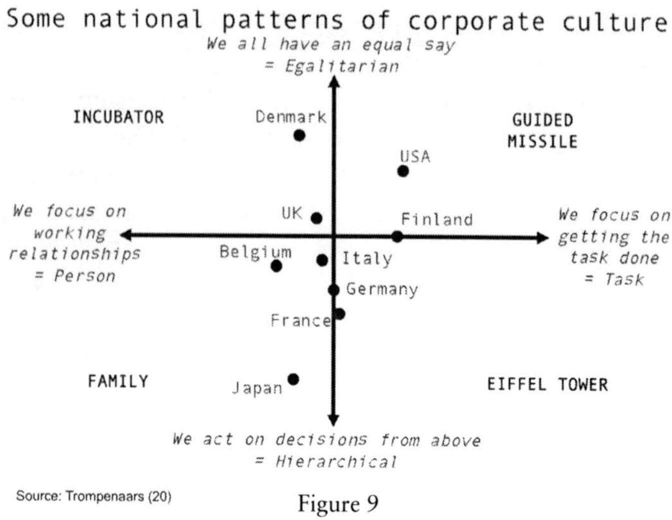

Figure 9

incubator. He then plots a range of different nationalities on this (Figure 9).

Hofstede's five dimensions

Geert Hofstede (21) took a different approach from Trompenaars. He identified five dimensions in which to assess cultural differences. These are:

- Power distance dimension (PDI) focuses on the degree of equality, or inequality, between people in the country's society
- Individualism-collectivism dimension (IDV) focuses on the degree the society reinforces individual or collective achievement and interpersonal relationships
- Uncertainty avoidance dimension (UAI) focuses on the level of tolerance for uncertainty and ambiguity within the society - i.e. unstructured situations

- Masculinity-femininity dimension (MAS) focuses on the degree the society reinforces, or does not reinforce, the traditional masculine work role model of male achievement, control and power
- Long-term orientation (LTO) focuses on the degree the society embraces, or does not embrace, long-term devotion to traditional, forward thinking values.

Each dimension is measured on a scale low (0) to high (100). The LTO dimension was added at a later stage and is not available for the countries that were analysed in the early stages. An example of how different cultures scored in these five dimensions is given in Figure 10.

Hofstede keeps his web site up to date showing the latest versions of his analysis (22) which includes data on an extensive list of countries.

Hofstede's 5 dimensions

	PDI	IDV	UAI	MAS	LTO
France	68	71	86	43	
Finland	33	63	59	26	
Great Britain	35	89	35	66	25
Germany FR	35	67	65	66	31
Hong Kong	68	25	29	57	96
Japan	54	46	92	95	80
India	77	48	40	56	61
USA	40	91	46	62	29

Source: Hofstede (21)

Figure 10

How can these approaches be used?

The key to using either or both of these approaches is to look at the relative positions of the two cultures being considered. The bigger the difference in a dimension, the greater is the chance of problems and challenges. The greatest value of these techniques lies in the creation of self-awareness and hence greater care when dealing with different nationalities and cultures.

How different cultures react

Does 'yes' mean 'yes'?

Culture differences can have a major impact on business. It is illuminating to compare an example of certain practices in Middle Eastern countries with the West, especially the United States. When negotiating in Western countries, the objective is to work towards a target of mutual understanding and agreement. Western people then shake hands when that agreement is reached. It is a cultural signal that the negotiations are complete and the parties can now start working together. In Middle Eastern countries much negotiation takes place prior to an agreement, signified by shaking hands. However, the deal is not complete in the Middle Eastern culture. In fact, it is a cultural sign that serious negotiations are just beginning. The different meaning of the handshake creates major problems when each party in a negotiation is operating under diametrically opposed rules and conventions.

Example 19

An experienced international executive worked for a company with operations in 14 countries. He said "I can ask the same question in each country and get exactly the same answer. They just mean fourteen different things".

Another example of different cultural interpretations is to understand when 'no' means 'no' and 'yes' means 'yes'. If someone is asked whether they know anything about a particular issue, an American might answer 'yes' if he or she can make an educated guess about it, whereas an Eastern European might answer 'no' unless he or she is absolutely sure (Example 19).

An oft-quoted dictum states that if an oriental businessman is asked in English if they agree with something, the first 'yes' means they have heard the words, the second 'yes' means that they understand the words and only the third 'yes' means that they agree with what has been said.

In these examples, none of the parties are wrong in what they say nor are they being misleading. It is simply a different cultural approach that can give rise to major misunderstandings. Before starting any significant dealings with another culture it is always useful to get a basic understanding of what the major differences in approach are between the two cultures, thus providing a useful aide memoire.

The level of relationship

It is important to recognise that social behaviour and business behaviour are different and that in some cultures it is not possible to have a business relationship without first establishing a personal relationship. Hofstede and Trompenaars provide an insight into these relative views of behaviour. Therefore, it is wise to look at both models before approaching a new culture.

In business dealings, the situation has an extra level of complexity. A key aspect of any multicultural business dealings is how each party sees the balance between three factors: the personal relationship between individuals; the overall relationship between the organisations and the specific deal relationship. The British and American approach tends to be focused on the deal, taking a short-term view until the relationship becomes based on trust but even then the deal takes priority.

The East Asian approach starts with building a personal relationship between the individuals concerned before any deal can be established. In this approach, the company is viewed almost as an intermediary that provides the product or service on behalf of the individual. The relationship between the organisations disappears if any of the key individuals change.

The third type of relationship puts the organisation first and is, therefore, usually the longest lasting. This approach is common, for example, in Southern and Eastern Europe. Such cultures have been traditionally family-centric and often businesses were family concerns so the organisations are treated rather like extended families.

It is important to understand the impact of the relationship level at the outset of any multicultural dealings because it sets the tone for everything that happens. It is not uncommon for western businessmen to seem rude to their Japanese or Chinese counterparts because they try to bypass the process of building a personal relationship in their hurry to get the deal done. In contrast, the same western businessmen may well feel that their oriental counterparts are wasting time and are not interested in doing business. Neither of these beliefs is true but the damage may already have been done.

An example of a cross-cultural view: the British view of Japan

There are many organisations that offer cross-cultural training between the main business nations. It is highly recommended that the cross-cultural views are understood before starting a new venture (Example 20). For longer term interactions, particularly those that involve immersion in the new culture for some staff, specific training should be given, focused on the culture as well as the language.

Example 20

The Managing Directors of the US and UK divisions of a multinational were talking over dinner. The American pointed out that the biggest difference between Americans and Brits was how they coped with failure. The British response was a stiff upper lip and to make sure they never try that again. The American response was to dust off their britches and say "gee that didn't work, let's try another way".

This example highlights a significant cultural difference in that European people in general are motivated away from concepts, in this case failure, whereas American people tend to be motivated towards concepts, in this case success. Such differences are subtle but important and need to be taken into consideration if a successful relationship is to be established.

It is particularly important between British and American organisations where the large areas of commonality, including language, mask significant differences in culture that can easily be overlooked.

Most cultures have a good understanding of the way in which they behave and of the elements that they see as core to their culture. When cultures interact, there are often specific differences in behaviour that create problems. As an example of how one culture views another, here are some of the key elements of Japanese culture that are significantly different when seen from a British or American standpoint (23):

- Uchi-Soto — Us and Them: The Japanese have been raised to think of themselves as part of a group and their group is always dealing with other groups.
- The Gaijin Complex: How Japanese view non-Japanese is always a subject of debate. Often there is a mixture of admiration, suspicion and most often a lot of nervousness about dealing with someone who doesn't look or act like the Japanese.
- Honne / Tatemae — The Real Mind & the Veneer: There is the way things are and the way we would like them to be - the reality and the facade.
- Osekkai! — Mind Your Own Business! Japanese society has two concurrent streams that frequently bump heads and the result is tension and stress. One current is protecting your own privacy, following your dream and doing things your own way at your own pace. The opposing current is the overwhelming social pressure to conform, follow the rules and make sure everyone else is in the same boat as you.
- Goatism — Giseisha / Urami — On Scapegoats, Victims, and Envy: The term 'goatism' comes from scapegoat and for a time was a frequently used buzzword by the Japanese. Japanese also have very positive traits but this is not one of them. In many instances, Japanese love to think of themselves as the victim.

- Amae - Dependency: Amae basically means dependence. In Japan, mavericks and lone-wolf types are very much frowned upon. When Japanese go off alone to a foreign country, many rapidly become insecure.
- Tate-shakai — The Vertical Society: Tate Shakai means a vertically structured society, like the military or a caste system.
- Shikata ga Nai / Gaman — You Can't Fight City Hall: Shikata ga nai means 'There's nothing you can do about it' and is often used by Japanese when they face a troubling situation they think they can't change.
- Nihonjinron / Kokusaika — We Japanese & Internationalization: It is almost always applied in a 'Japanese and everyone else' kind of way. Japan is the centre of the world and if you buy a map of the world don't be surprised to find Japan in the middle of it.
- The Iron Triangle and the Empty Centre or The Buck Never Stops: These terms are the lowest common denominators of how things run in Japan. The Iron Triangle is the Japanese System: the politicians, Big Business/Special Interests and the bloated bureaucracy. So who runs the country? None of them, really: each is engaged in a tug-of-war for its own interests.

Some sources have suggested that two out of three mergers, acquisitions and alliances between organisations in different cultures do not achieve anywhere near the expected benefits that prompted the venture (24). Given the potential for large differences between what can be at first sight similar cultures, this is not a surprising outcome. Even with a major effort on cultural training, it is unlikely that the success rate will be high. The key to success is probably in establishing a series of strong personal relationships between individuals at various levels in the organisations but this is not something that can be forced.

Impact on a board

When these culture differences are put in the context of decision making by a multicultural board, they can lead to significant and potentially damaging conflicts. Not having a multicultural board can also lead to seriously flawed decisions under certain circumstances. However it is imperative that multicultural boards accommodate the relevant differences.

Even multicultural boards are generally dominated by people from the company's home country with a limited number of individuals from other countries. The risk is that a single director from a different background will be isolated from the rest of the board. Their reaction is normally either to remain an outsider (and, therefore, be ineffective) or to over-compensate, which can irritate the other board members. It is a very difficult balance to achieve. The onus must be on the majority to understand, accept and work with the minority.

Implementing board decisions

The board must also be cognisant of the way in which its decisions will be accepted in its different operating regions. For example, it is clear from Trompenaars' work that there would be a very different reaction to a dictate by the board from a subsidiary in Japan to that from a subsidiary in Denmark. The former might take it very seriously whereas the latter might look at it as merely an interesting suggestion.

In order to make the board's decisions work effectively, someone has to act as a cultural bridge. It can be a primary role for any foreign board member, otherwise the CEO must take responsibility. Cultural bridging has a significant impact on the way in which the board communicates its goals, strategy and decisions throughout the organisation. It needs to work with the executive management team, especially in foreign subsidiaries, to ensure that the message is shaped for each culture to achieve the required outcome.

The CEO of a multinational and multicultural organisation needs to be very aware of the impact of culture differences in order to manage them successfully. It is too easy to assume that globalisation as a goal is strong enough to pull people together. A coherent organisation can only be achieved using a bottom-up approach based on an understanding of the differences so their impact on the success and effectiveness of the organisation is optimised, reinforcing the dictum 'think global, act local'.

8. Board issues

Chapter 6 focused on individual personalities and how these affect the board. This chapter looks at the way in which the board interacts and what it needs as a team in order to deliver effective performance.

Gaps in the board

The relative importance of various functions and people often change progressively as an organisation evolves. This evolution can create gaps in what was previously a well-balanced board (Figure 11). The chairman should take the lead in reviewing the board on a regular basis in

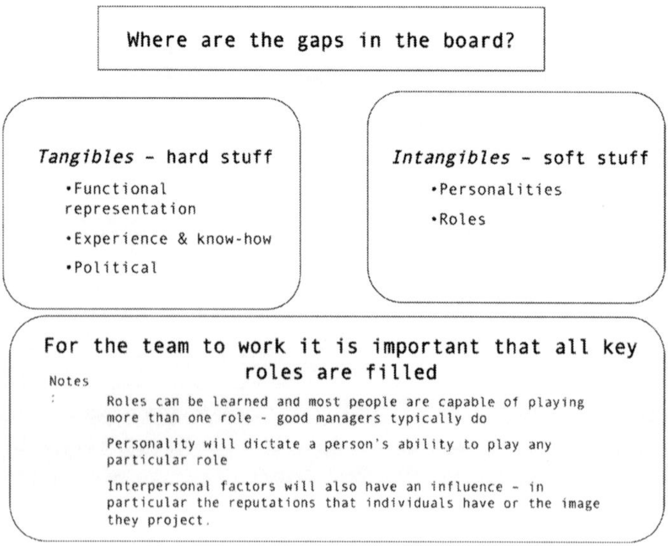

Figure 11

order to maintain balance. For example, factors such as political contacts and influence can be neutralised in the event of a change of government.

A board must not only have all the skills required to fulfil its function but it must also be able to operate effectively as a team. Any gaps in either aspect make it prone to error and misjudgement. It is, therefore, imperative that gaps are identified and filled as soon as possible to provide an adequate safeguard for the organisation.

Tangibles

The first step is to understand what shape the board needs in order to be most effective. There are two dimensions: functional scope and risk.

The tangible elements mean that the experience of board members enables them to understand and discuss the main functional aspects of the organisation - sales, production, finance etc. They also ensure that the board has the right depth of experience to be able to identify and address problems and risk areas. In its external–facing role, the board should have the right level of contacts and political influence to maximise opportunities for the organisation.

Most boards are very good at ensuring that the tangible aspects are well covered, although problems may arise in harnessing these skills. For example, the organisation may wish to use the skills of non-executives in a more active mode which then conflicts with their time commitments. A sound recruitment process can ensure that new recruits have the right combination of skills and experience coupled with the ability to dedicate enough time to meet anticipated requirements.

The nature of the organisation can be analysed and mapped to identify key functional aspects and their priorities at a certain stage in its development. The key skills should be represented on the board to ensure that it has sufficient knowledge to ask probing questions and to understand the answers. For immature organisations, it is helpful to look forward and map how the functional priorities would be expected to change over the next few years so that the board can be prepared.

A similar analysis and map can also be prepared for risk areas. Greater experience is needed on the board to counter the perceived areas of risk. A lower priority function may be associated with high levels of risk and vice versa. For example, it is not uncommon for early stage technology companies to focus on the technology risks but fail to address the financial and sales risks with the same vigour. This can lead to serious financial issues, often shortage of cash, despite the company overcoming major technical hurdles.

It is important to recognise that even mature organisations continue to evolve and, therefore, the functional and risk maps need to be re-assessed on a regular basis - certainly before any significant change to the board.

Intangibles

The intangible elements include the personalities, the roles of the individuals, the relationships that form between board members and those that board members form with key stakeholders.

As discussed in chapter 6, the choice of role that people play is normally in response to an instinctive reaction to the environment. However, people can make proactive choices about how they behave and this flexibility provides scope to cover gaps in board roles as they appear. It is essential to fill all key roles. The chairman should know the board members' personalities well enough to understand what roles they are capable of occupying. He or she can then take the lead in getting them to adopt appropriate roles to ensure gaps are filled and that the board is balanced.

Common understanding

Effective boards share a common understanding of what they want the organisation to achieve, of how it can be achieved and of how the board should work (Figure 12). This unity of purpose provides a bond that supports good board dynamics. In contrast, the lack of such a coherent view can be a major cause of conflict in the board.

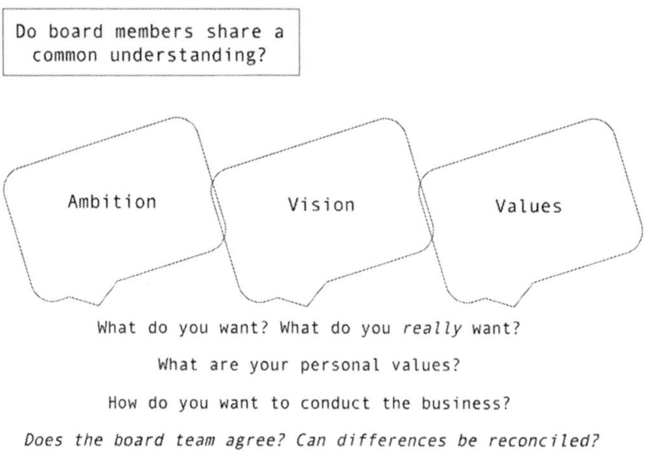

Figure 12

The shared understanding needs to cover three main areas:

- ambition
- vision
- values.

Ambition is the will to succeed – the energy that drives the business forward. This can break down when poor board dynamics make a board member focus his or her attention on other interests or when a non-executive director regards his or her role as a sinecure.

The board should share a common vision for the future of the company and the path that it needs to take. An example of the vision breaking down is in family owned companies where the younger shareholders want to drive the business forward but the older shareholders just want a safe pension. A similar problem arises when an investor wants to drive the company to optimise their overall portfolio rather than optimise the company itself.

Shared values tend to be far more personal. They represent a common way of thinking and of approaching problems. A shared view not only makes it easier and quicker for the board to agree but also provides a common ground for reconciling any differences that arise (Example 21).

Example 21

An engineering group was run by a small board who all happened by chance to be committed Christians. Whilst their religious views did not dictate their business decisions, they recognised that their shared values generated a unity of purpose which made the board run smoothly.

A similar logic ought to apply to family businesses but the scope for internecine strife can often outweigh the commonality of view, particularly for later generation companies, based on the principle that you can choose your friends but you cannot choose your relatives.

A common set of values often derives from a similar upbringing and it may be a key factor in driving family businesses forward. There is an implication that it can be more difficult to achieve unity of purpose when the board contains people from different backgrounds and sometimes different cultures. The counter is that the mix of backgrounds and cultures is more likely to ensure an open discussion and to make the shared purpose explicit.

There is a marked contrast between 'unity of purpose' and 'group think'. The former reflects a common way of addressing issues rather than a common view of them.

Dysfunctional behaviour

Dysfunctional behaviour can undermine any board. There are three main sources of such behaviour that can affect the board as a whole: functional deficiencies, individual behaviour and group culture (Figure 13).

Straightforward functional deficiencies are inexcusable. It must be recognised that the functional expertise

Figure 13

required by the board evolves as an organisation matures but this can be planned for. More complex deficiencies can usually be identified by using the Frame Model analysis described earlier.

Many of the individual behaviour issues are outlined in Chapter 6 on personalities and roles. Here we concentrate on group behaviour and group culture that can impact on board performance.

Group problems arise in two forms; those that affect part of the board and those that affect the whole board. The latter are far more difficult and the challenge is how to identify that a problem has arisen. The board members themselves are not likely recognise that there is a problem, without a major event that is obvious to all concerned, because they are part of the problem. In all cases, it is preferable to persuade the offending board members of the error of their ways although sometimes the problem is so entrenched that replacement may be the best option.

Bullying. Bullying is a complex interaction. It needs a target to be bullied and the rest of the group to allow it to happen. Given the fact that board members should be strong people, it ought to be uncommon. The key is that the rest of the board must recognise when bullying is taking place and act, through the chairman, to stop it. The Bully should be warned and, if the problem persists, replaced.

Group think. Group think is a common problem because board members can spend a lot of time telling outsiders how good the organisation is, in order to allow room for manoeuvre and to protect their positions. This can lead to them believing their own hype and ignoring deficiencies. It is a failure of the board's monitoring role.

Classic problems that can arise due to group think are: to underestimate the threat posed by competitors, to ignore risk areas and to overestimate the commitment of both customers and suppliers. The solution to group think problems is to maintain an effective and objective monitoring role. It can be hard to break out of this type of problem and it usually requires a very strong individual or a shock to the organisation in order to achieve it.

Over-conservatism. It is uncommon for boards to be naturally over-conservative. They may have become so as a reaction to a previous problem, especially in certain cultures, e.g. the British stiff upper lip. Essentially, the group becomes driven by fear of failure and the monitoring role dominates. The worry is that new board members, who are naturally risk-averse, are brought in as a reaction, thereby compounding the problem. Strong leadership, especially by the chairman, is essential to move the board back to a better balanced approach to challenges and risks. Strong strategic thinking can be very helpful in overcoming this problem.

Blasé culture. Blasé culture indulges in excessive risk taking due to weaknesses in both the monitoring and operations roles. The most common cause is when the culture does not develop along with the company. All start-ups and early stage companies are inherently risky. As they mature, the acceptable risk levels reduce. If the board's culture does not evolve then it can easily become blasé.

Acceptable risk levels can change very quickly, for example when a venture capital funded company floats on the stock exchange. Public companies need much tighter risk control and predictability. If the approach of the board does not make a step change to reflect this then it can seriously damage the company at a critical time in its development.

Usually, the problem results from a few board members. Such individuals should be dissuaded or replaced once the problem is diagnosed. The chairman must never allow a whole board to become blasé. If he or she does so, the solution is to replace the chairman. If the solution is deep-rooted then it may be necessary to change the CEO as well, however, changing both in rapid succession will ring alarm bells to any outsider watching the organisation.

Delusional thinking. Delusional thinking can arise when the board allows the preconceptions of some of its members to guide its overall decisions. Once again, this is a failure of the monitoring role. A common cause is where the creator of the business concept, or the inventor of the core technology, is on the board and he or she has an unshatterable belief in the strength of the core idea. During the very early stages of an innovative business, everyone has to buy into the belief to some extent but it must be tempered by objectivity as soon as possible.

It is common for such creative individuals to take on the Specialist role in the team as the organisation develops. When this happens, it is important to ensure that the board has someone available, although not necessarily on the board, who can provide an objective assessment of the Specialist's area. In such cases, Specialists may be necessary evils on the board so they must be brought into line as replacement may not be an option.

Blame culture. Blame cultures usually centre on one or two individuals who are motivated by fear of failure and exert undue influence on the rest of the board. In practice, the result is similar to being over-conservative. However, a blame culture is far more damaging to board relationships and dynamics because it undermines those who are being blamed. It is a long-term problem because it is driven by motivation rather than a reaction to an issue.

Fear of failure is not an intrinsically bad motivation for a board member as it can make them good at the monitoring and operations roles. Blame for its own sake is always an issue. The problem typically arises when there is a clash of motivations across the board so it is difficult for each party to understand what the other is trying to achieve. Sometimes one party then drives the other to a more extreme reaction. The easy solution is to dissuade or remove the person who drives the blame culture but this is not necessarily the right solution. If the problem is a result of a clash of two motivations then board dynamics suggest that the more extreme person is replaced.

Empire building. Empire building occurs when one individual, typically an Autocratic type, takes too much control and uses the organisation to build a power base. It is more than just a personality trait because, as in the case of bullying, other members of the board have to allow it to happen. If the culprit is a normal board member then the chairman should not have allowed it. Questions must be raised by the other board members as to their performance as well.

If the culprit is either the CEO or the chairman then the solution may require strong measures. Under these circumstances, it may be necessary for the senior non-executive director to approach the major shareholders to seek their support in forcing through a change. Sometimes the culprit may be the representative of a major shareholder in which case the chairman may need to approach the shareholder to encourage them to admonish or replace the individual.

Organisational bystanders. 'Organisational bystanders' is a term used by Gerstein (25) to describe the behaviour when members of a group can see a major problem but allow themselves to be shouted down by the other members of the group or to not press the issue because of a sense of loyalty. The classic example that Gerstein cites is of the NASA space shuttle disaster where a senior manager predicted the fatal problem, was told by his colleagues that NASA did not have problems like that and so went quiet.

Such behaviour happens on boards as well and is a form of group think that may be used by part of the board against another board member. In terms of the Frame Model, it is an overuse of the drive role. The counter is for the chairman, or the party flagging the risk, to ensure that any such risk area is noted officially in the board papers. Given the legal responsibilities of board members, it is very hard for them not to accept liability for something about which they have been given reasonable warning.

Board performance

The classic principle of 'measure, monitor, modify' applies to boards as much as to any other process. As with all teams, it can be difficult to distinguish between the performance of the board and the performance of the organisation. This requires a complex set of measures, ideally combining suitable metrics with benchmarking to give a balanced and objective assessment of performance.

Metrics – leading & lagging indicators

Metrics are sometimes described as 'leading' or 'lagging' indicators. The easiest ones to measure usually assess the performance that has been achieved. These are lagging indicators. They can be very detailed but they show that there was a problem in the past rather than predict ones in the future. The classic example is a financial metric such as profit which is both detailed and quantifiable.

Some indicators look at the situation at a particular point in time. These can give a good measure of the specific situation but find it difficult to distinguish between, for example, a good performance in a difficult situation and a poor performance in a good situation.

For boards, some of the most helpful indicators are leading because they highlight where problems might arise and, therefore, enable avoidance. By nature these are much softer and less rigorous metrics because they look at the shape of things rather than quantify details with great accuracy. They also tend to be broader in scope.

Overall board performance assessment works best with a combination of both types of metric such as:

- Leading indicators:
  - Board dynamics assessment, including the Frame Model, motivation analysis and, where appropriate, psychometric tests
  - Mapping functional skills against requirements
  - Board governance assessment based on the Combined Code
  - Strategy execution monitoring
- Lagging indicators:
  - Financial performance against budget and, for a public company, against analysts' forecasts
  - Quality measures, especially customer feedback
  - Employee feedback and climate
  - Achievement of the objectives of the strategic plan

The assessment of leading indicators often highlights areas for improvement that can have a rapid impact on both leading and lagging metrics. The links to the lagging indicators are much harder to relate to specific improvements. Lagging indicators use information that will probably be available to investors and stakeholders who will make their own decisions based on it. Using earlier indicators, even though they are softer, gives the board a much better chance of improving its own performance before it is made to do so by external forces.

Using a balanced set of metrics to obtain a view of board performance gives a strong framework in which to assess the performance of individual board members. The leading indicators underline the role of individuals and the team whilst the lagging indicators relate to the performance of the team and the organisation.

Benchmarking

Benchmarking requires a mechanism for comparison which is only practical if there are meaningful and repeatable metrics that can be applied. Lagging indicators, such as financial performance, are easy for companies to derive and monitor. Leading indicators, such as board dynamics, focus on the internal workings of the board. They may not relate to other boards and are harder to measure.

The acid test for a board is benchmarking against similar companies but this is hard to separate from the performance of the organisation. Investors are used to comparing the performance of companies. They do not have a means of assessing the boards per se. As a compromise they use the track record of directors in terms of the performance of the various companies in which they have worked. This is a very sensible approach but it is only meaningful if the directors concerned have worked in a number of companies whose performance is available to the investor. It works well for large public companies whose directors need a strong track record in order to be appointed. Investors in unquoted companies find this approach much harder to use. As a general rule, investors in the smaller UK companies are very intolerant of any failure. They effectively employ a 'one strike and you are out' policy, which is consistent with being motivated by fear of failure but is neither benchmarking nor even a comparison.

Corporate governance assessment

A number of consultancies offer corporate governance assessments. They work with companies to help them assess and improve their performance in this area. For example, one organisation (26) has developed a set of metrics for assessing the performance of a board based on the Combined Code of Corporate Governance. It is a leading indicator which provides a quantifiable result and one that is repeatable when assessed by trained staff.

The quantification not only allows the board to improve itself but also to be compared with the boards of similar organisations. This metric is unlikely to be made public but the assessment team can and should build a database of results to enable meaningful comparison. It enables the assessment team to tell a board how they compare with similar organisations without the need to release sensitive information, thereby providing a reasonable benchmark.

An assessment of this type is helpful in ensuring that the processes and structure of the board follow good practice but it does not address the issues concerning the way that people interact. It works best for large public companies for whom the Combined Code was developed and whose boards comprise highly experienced board members. The background of the directors ought to ensure that the boards of these high profile companies are less likely to suffer from dynamics problems but there are many cases of even very large quoted businesses being damaged by them.

The balance is the other way round for SMEs where board dynamics are usually the most important factors, reflecting the narrower experience of the board members. For such businesses, following good corporate governance guidelines is desirable but not critical. The two approaches should be regarded as complementary tools to maximise the effectiveness of the board.

The balanced board

A critical question is 'what does a balanced and effective board look like?' The elements that need to be balanced are function, risk, experience and personal dynamics, including communication. The first step is to get the board structure right, preferably using the mapping processes for function and risk outlined above. A sound recruitment process can then build on this by ensuring that board members have the right personal skills and style to make the board work effectively. An important criterion is how individuals react to new challenges. Some members of the board should be chosen because they react well. Whilst it does not enable the board to expect the unexpected, it does give the board a much stronger position when the unexpected happens.

Optimising board structure and recruitment ought to create a board that is balanced and well matched to the needs of the organisation. These optimisations can be performed by people from outside the board looking in. The next steps are ongoing internal processes. It is important to provide a mechanism for reviewing and balancing the board dynamics, backed up by psychometric tests where appropriate. This is done most effectively from inside the board with the chairman taking the lead. The goal is to achieve 'constructive disagreement', balancing the ability to present a cogent opinion with the ability to understand and analyse the opinions of others.

Putting theory into practice

So far the discussion has been an empirical assessment of what a board needs in order to operate effectively, both in terms of the roles and skills that are required to succeed, and some behavioural elements that can make it fail. The critical issue is how these models can be put into practice to protect the interests of the organisation.

The issue is complicated by the fact that a board is a closed group. Therefore, the people who are in a position to observe what is happening are themselves part of the group and may also be part of the problem. The identification of potential problems brings into play an important element of normal team operation: watch out for others and others watch out for you.

There are three steps that should be taken to help a board make effective use of these concepts:

- Tailored awareness and training
- Refining the recruitment process
- Monitoring board interactions.

These three steps are discussed below.

Awareness & training

The first practical step is to make board members aware of the two core concepts; firstly, the interplay between the four roles of the Frame Model - strategy, drive, monitor and operations - and secondly, the impact of board dynamics on multi-faceted personalities. Being aware of these concepts and being able to discuss them with other board members creates a solid framework for good practice.

It is essential that the chairman and at least one other director, preferably the senior non-executive, have a sound understanding of and appreciate the principles of board dynamics as a powerful complement to the in-depth practical experience that they should already have. Training a second board member provides a safety net in case the chairman is part of the problem. All other board members should be aware of, and be open to discussion about, these principles. Awareness is often sufficient to enable problems to be identified and resolved before they become significant.

Once board members have been made aware of the principles, they will soon recognise board dynamics issues caused by their colleagues. It is far more difficult for them to recognise problems in themselves so the awareness training needs to ensure that the board members are willing to listen to criticism. Board dynamics can then be discussed as part of the general mentoring of directors. It should certainly be an element of the appraisal process.

Impact on board recruitment

The second step is for the chairman and the chair of the nominations committee to consider the four roles of the Frame Model when recruiting new board members. It is standard practice to recruit board members based on their experience both functionally and at board level. It is less common for personality types to be taken into consideration during the recruitment process other than meeting the potential colleagues for a 'fireside chat' to see if they can work together.

The Frame Model provides a basis for defining the preferred personal styles of new board members to support the functional capabilities and experience that they are expected to bring. The two aspects are not wholly independent. For example, it would not be sensible to try to find a corporate strategy director who was strong in the operations role. If such disparities arise then further changes might be needed to the board with either additional non-executives being required or by identifying that an existing board member is upsetting the balance of the board.

The normal recruitment process, combining both formal and informal interviews, is often insufficient because it can show a narrow, and usually amicable, part of the individual's personality. Probably the most important aspect of the interview process is what questions the candidates ask and how they ask them as this gives insight into their way of thinking, their ability to listen and their manner. The interviewer should attempt to learn enough about the candidate's approach to determine which role or roles they are likely to adopt. Where there is a potential overlap for these roles with existing board members then it is advisable to get those board members to meet the candidate, preferably on a one-to-one basis, to determine how well they might work together. It must be remembered that it is desirable for the board to have two people who are strong in the four roles – the key is to make sure that they can interact in a constructive manner.

It is difficult to identify potential board dynamics issues in an interview situation as all parties are likely to be on their best behaviour. Deliberately challenging the candidate, in a non-aggressive manner, is a reasonable interview tactic if used judiciously. If done correctly, it can give an insight into the candidate's personal approach and how he or she might interact with the rest of the board. An important element of the recruitment phase is to talk to referees, ideally including the chairman of a board on which the candidate has sat, as this can provide first-hand knowledge from a broad range of situations.

Psychometric testing, even at a simple level, can help to identify the range of the candidate's personality. It enables a better balanced board to be established and gives the chairman an insight that can forewarn him or her of potential dynamics issues. The problem is that many board candidates would see this as odd unless it is something that is done for all management staff as a matter of policy.

Monitoring dynamics

The critical elements in resolving board dynamics problems are to identify and analyse the core issues. With a sound knowledge of board dynamics, the chairman should be able to spot potential problems as they arise and then intervene directly, during the board meeting if necessary, to ensure the board operates effectively. This intervention may be either to ensure that all parties express their ideas and opinions or to challenge the ways in which those opinions are expressed in order to achieve a balanced discussion. The process becomes much easier if all board members are familiar with the principles and so appreciate what the chairman is trying to achieve. Methods of resolving problems are discussed in detail in the following chapter.

Dynamics issues can also arise in a board that previously worked effectively because of changes either in circumstances or in the relationships between board members. New issues then drive the individuals towards using less desirable facets of their personalities. However, it is more common for these issues to develop either because no notice was taken of potential personality clashes during the recruitment process or when someone new is appointed to the board.

Impact on communication

Effective communication is critical to the success of any group. In order to fulfil its responsibilities, a board must take all reasonable steps to identify risks and opportunities. This means that all appropriate issues need to be brought before the board and discussed where there are any doubts or alternative views. Poor board dynamics can be a major barrier not only to any discussion but also to getting things discussed. In turn, poor communications are the most common early symptom of board dynamics problems and require careful monitoring to enable the identification and resolution of such issues.

Information sharing

In order to have an open, in-depth board discussion it is essential that all board members not only have sufficient information about the issue but also have had enough time to consider its implications and seek supporting information as required. Because different people take different lengths of time to develop their views, it is important that all key information is made available early. There should be no surprises at a board meeting, either in terms of the level or the scope of information, because these create barriers to sound decision making.

As discussed in Chapter 5, a key step is to have clear, thorough and accurate board papers available in a timely manner which then puts the onus on board members to read the papers thoroughly before the meeting. If any further information or issues arise after the board papers are distributed then the board must be informed as soon as possible to allow time for consideration.

What the listener hears

The critical element in communication is not what the speaker says but what the listener hears. Based on the Frame Model, a good board utilises the constructive tension between strong characters who have different styles and approaches. It can, therefore, be quite challenging to ensure that the right message is received. The greatest potential for communication issues within the Frame Model lies between the strategy and operations roles because it is common for people who naturally see the big picture to be poor at details and vice versa.

A board needs members who can make balanced judgements so it is important that each director has sufficient breadth of understanding to appreciate the opposite viewpoint. Too many 'narrow' people will cause a problem on a board as it makes communication far more difficult. It is important to have at least one person, often the chairman, who can help to bridge the understanding gap between opposing styles and roles when some board members are being intransigent or just having a bad day.

The burden lies with the chairman to ensure that critical issues have been discussed thoroughly, that no significant aspects have been overlooked and that the whole board has the same understanding of the issue. This does not mean that all board members will have taken a balanced view but they will have been given the opportunity to do so.

The impact of board dynamics

A common characteristic of board dynamics problems is that the listener simply stops listening to another's views, either because of the way in which these are expressed or because of the personality of the individual who is expressing them. The listener effectively switches into another personality facet that is inappropriate for board level work, making it difficult to reach a balanced decision, not just for the board member who stops listening but also for the rest of the board because of the tension that is created.

If such a situation arises then the chairman should appoint a suitable member of the board to provide a succinct summary of both sides of the point at issue. The summary assists the non-conflicting board members in making a balanced judgement and can help to diffuse tension between the conflicting parties. If the conflict recurs then the chairman needs take remedial action as discussed in the following chapter.

Ensuring the right level and balance of communication is critical in resolving dynamics issues. The chairman must identify early in the discussion whether there are potential and critical points of contention. If there are no areas of disagreement then the chairman needs to feel comfortable that the issue has been discussed in appropriate depth. If there are points of contention then he or she should aim to elicit enough information about the opposing views to allow a decision to be made.

When board dynamics play a part in the discussion then it is likely that the parties will either over-argue their case, providing too much detail and confusing the issue, or will say too little, assuming that the answer is self-evident. Elicitation by the chairman requires a balance between these two extremes. Encouraging the conflicting parties to provide the right level of information helps them to focus on the message they are trying to get across rather than the personality issues, thereby helping to defuse the problem.

9. Building & maintaining an effective board

Managing change

As organisations evolve, their priorities and focus change and the level of involvement of the investors also changes. Classic models of business evolution include:

- Technology companies moving from a research-based technology concept to a mature commercial entity
- Product companies starting in a garage and expanding to multinational status
- Retail companies starting with a small number of shops and developing into a large chain.

There are many examples of technology start-ups, including university spin-outs. HP, the major electronics company, is famous for starting out in a garage. This has happened to a number of well-known names. The more interesting retail examples include those with a particular focus. For example, based on a core vision of an ethical market opportunity, Body Shop evolved relatively quickly into a retail chain with 250 shops. Many of the big retail chains started with a single shop, although it usually took a long time for them to build up to the rapid growth phase.

The founders of businesses are often visionaries who bring in acolytes to share and develop their vision. The businesses then develop into hard-nosed commercial entities with a clearly defined market niche - a process involving huge cultural changes within the company. This development is often associated with radical changes to the board and the management team. A classic problem is when the founders of such companies cling on to their vision and to control of the company well beyond their usefulness, causing major confrontations. Founders who can grow along with their businesses are a rare breed, as discussed later in this chapter.

For businesses which grow and evolve, it is possible that the whole board will need to be replaced more than once to ensure it has the right skills at the right time to meet the needs of the organisation. This evolution can be anticipated and planned for at the outset and agreed with the board members who can then be adequately motivated and compensated for their contribution to the company.

The board must evolve to ensure it has the right skill set to manage the current and anticipated issues facing the organisation. It should have a forward view that takes account of investment cycles. The board is not a static entity and neither are the directors. They should expect to have a 'shelf-life' that is driven by the needs of the organisation. It is possible that directors can use different aspects of their personalities and take on roles that grow to match the needs of the company but this is frequently not the case.

The renewal term for NEDs provides a useful opportunity to review their fit with the board and the roles that they might take. Too often, the renewal process is almost a rubber-stamping exercise. In many private companies there is no renewal term at all. This leads to stasis and can be very damaging when the company faces new challenges of which the established board lacks experience.

As non-executives are often of 'a certain age', some may become far more interested in maintaining their income rather than fulfilling the real job of a director: the 'comfort factor' creeps in. The Combined Code recommends that NEDs should not have their term renewed more than once. This is eminently sensible unless there are very powerful reasons to the contrary. An easy response to the need to change a NED is to pick another from a small clique of trusted individuals. This looks like a safe option but may not expand the board's knowledge base. Limiting the selection process in this way can itself be a significant risk in a dynamic situation.

Organisation dynamics

Growth stages

Every organisation progresses through different stages in its development:

In the **start-up** phase, the business is normally focused on its vision, shaping its business concept and requiring unquestioning support and nurturing by its management and shareholders. It has a total belief in its own view of the future.

In the **pre-revenue** phase, the concept becomes a business and starts taking steps towards the outside world. It has to learn to change its behaviour to accommodate the constraints imposed by reality. Future plans start to change to reflect the needs of the real world rather than those the company expected as a start-up.

In the **early revenue** phase, the business begins to believe it has an existence that is independent from that of its investors. As the revenues grow and the company moves to profitability, the struggle for independence can become fierce. The company also becomes increasingly accountable for its performance. High growth brings with it a series of difficult challenges and the company needs the experience that the board ought to provide to help it cope with these.

In the **mature** phase, the business is fully self-supporting. The relationship between the business and the investors becomes arms-length but the price of this is full accountability in terms of delivering results rather than promises.

The evolution of a business is shown in a classic form in Figure 14. The figure shows the progressive shift over time from the initial focus on the strategic vision to the impact of the real world. As the business matures, an important factor is to get the right balance between

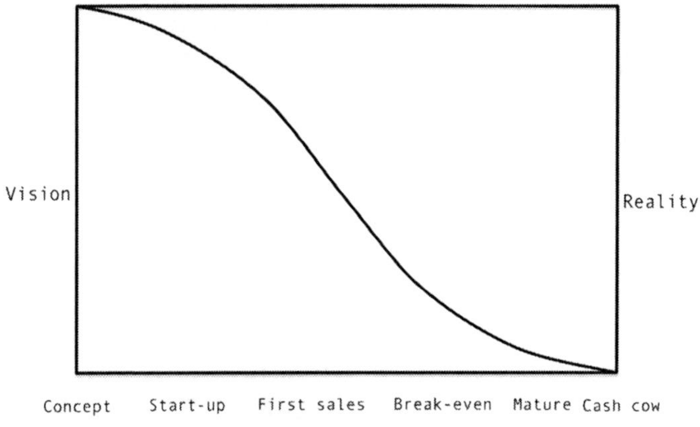

Figure 14

vision and reality in a mature business and to understand the implications of that balance. The vertical axes could easily be re-labelled as 'Strategy' instead of 'Vision' and 'Operations' instead of 'Reality', reflecting a strong correlation with the Frame Model, as discussed below. It is important to note that the mature phase is not at the right hand edge of the scale as such organisations need to have sufficient vision for renewal and reinvention. This is an area where good NEDs can be especially useful.

The nature and approach of the board has to change to reflect the development of the business. Using the terminology of transactional analysis, the basis of the relationship between the board and the company changes from parent-child to parent-adult (27). The board members must, therefore, be able to change their style and role to match the changing needs of the company or they themselves should be changed.

Board dynamics develop from the relationships between individual board members. As change is the major threat to any relationship, it is clear that maintaining effective dynamics is very challenging in a growing business. The critical issue is that the board dynamics can become most problematic at a time when the business needs the most help from the board.

The board needs to be aware of and manage change. The chairman ought to regularly review the balance of functional skills and experience on the board to make sure it reflects the current and anticipated needs of the organisation rather than its historic needs. He or she needs to monitor the impact of these changes on the board dynamics and take action to prevent the effectiveness of the board being impaired. The action may vary from simple intervention, through mentoring and external coaching to replacing board members in difficult cases.

The external view of the Frame Model

The four roles of the Frame Model can also be regarded as two pairs of opposing forces trying to pull the organisation, not just the board, in different directions. The status quo between the four forces reflects the overall direction of the organisation which is directly related to its stage of development. The external view of the Frame Model can then be represented in a very different form. Figure 15 shows the four forces in action. In this example, they are balanced and of equal significance, which would be the case for a company in the middle of its life. Strategy and drive are necessary to take the business into the future with new opportunities. These

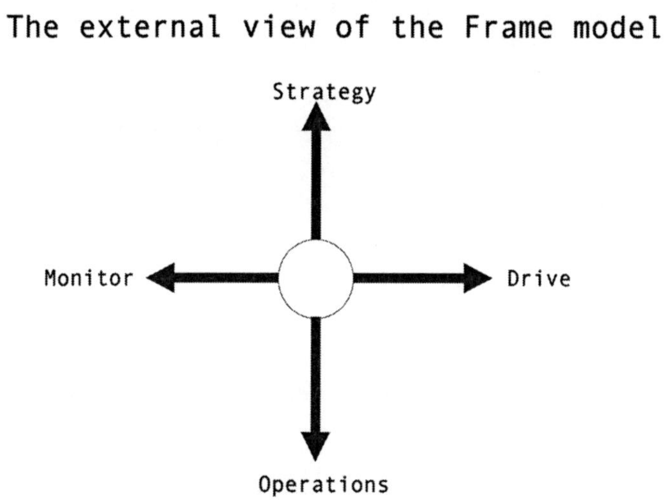

Figure 15

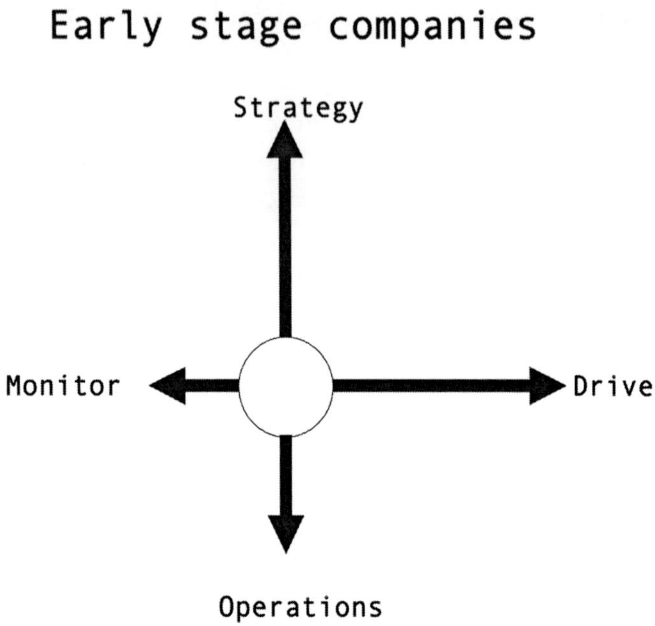

Figure 16

forces are balanced by a good focus on day-to-day operational issues and sound risk management from the monitor.

The balance between the opposing forces is very different at the extremes of an organisation's existence. Figure 16 depicts an early stage company where the main emphasis is on the strategic vision and the energy that is required to get it off the ground. Operations take on a lesser role because the products are immature and the monitor role is less significant because the key risk is in ensuring that the strategic vision is clear.

Towards the end of an organisation's life, the balance of the four forces pulls in the opposite direction. When a business becomes a cash cow (Figure 17), all the strategic and drive forces need to do is to protect the niche that is being milked. The operations dimension becomes critical. It might focus on details such as driving cost out of the product and ensuring continuity of supply for materials. Monitoring is also a vital role which examines how best to defend the niche against threats that might attack it and in making the critical decision as to when the niche has lost its value.

The organisation dynamics are closely connected to the board dynamics but it is the latter that is the dominant element. The essential factor is that the balance of the four external forces, which changes as

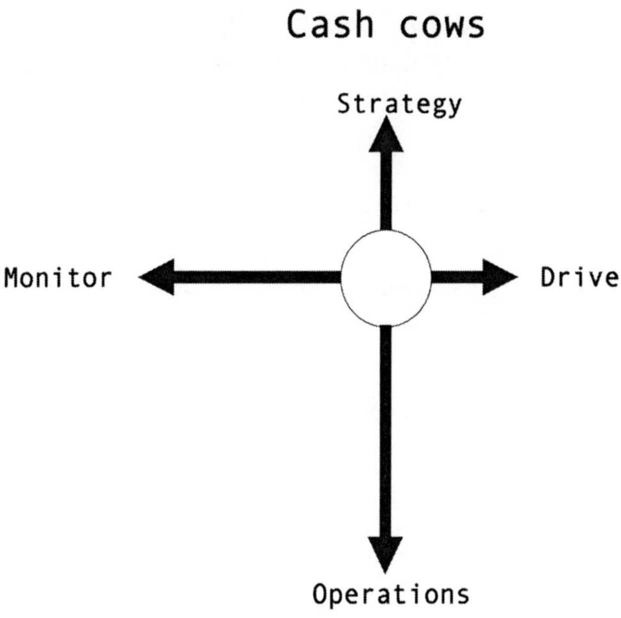

Figure 17

the organisation evolves, must be reflected in the balance of the four roles within the board. The balance between the four forces/roles of the Frame Model is determined by the stage of the organisation's development in the short to medium term. The composition of the board can be set up to reflect the required balance and must develop with the organisation. The board can then provide the overall force to drive the evolution of the business. An over-conservative board in an early stage company and an over aggressive board in a late stage company can both be very damaging indeed.

The founder syndrome

Founders must have plenty of drive and vision to enable them to tackle the huge challenges of starting up an organisation. For them to succeed, they often have an unwavering belief in their own business concept coupled with tunnel vision so they do not see the barriers that would daunt lesser mortals.

Founders are likely to be creative individuals with a low fear of failure (Example 22). They want to be in control of their 'baby' and expect to be on the board as CEO or possibly chairman. They also want to reap the huge rewards that their concept deserves. If it does not then, in their view, it is probably due to the failure of others in its implementation.

Example 22

A clever, well-educated scientist, known as the Doctor, started a series of different, innovatively-based companies, all using VC money. The concepts underlying each company were technically sophisticated and not easily grasped by non-technical experts – a factor he relied upon. In each case, the Doctor insisted on recruiting a large team of bright, young scientists to develop his ideas further as soon as money was forthcoming. However, he invariably lost sight of the concept of shareholder value, preferring to indulge his blue-sky ideas well beyond what was necessary to establish 'proof of principle'.

In one of the bigger, longer-lasting companies, no project management was used and hence there were no deadlines. This was despite having set up an application engineering facility in a different continent (in a city he liked) to productise the concept. The Doctor insisted on retaining the role of CEO on the board until the VCs, in deep frustration, decreed that an outside CEO be recruited and support in project management be introduced. It was soon apparent to the newcomers that making this a viable business was going to be very challenging, though this did not worry the Doctor. He just saw the VCs as financial backers for his personal development activity.

The company which had, at the time of the arrival of the new CEO and support, some 100 employees in three continents, operated for a further year and was sold, never having broken even. It was then stripped of its intellectual property (IP) - the only thing that was valuable about it. The VC lost a significant sum of money.

The Doctor continued to attract funding from other VCs for other ideas, thanks to his undoubted selling skills and powers of persuasion.

Theirs are necessary and admirable skills but they do not fit easily into what should be a balanced board. When the founder is a major shareholder then they have sufficient control to feel comfortable. The problems arise progressively when external shareholders become involved, often in the form of venture capital or private equity players, and the founder loses control of the company.

Normally founders will not sell a controlling interest to someone whose interests do not appear to be fully aligned with their own and only sell if the need for funds to fulfil the potential of the business, i.e. the founder's vision, is paramount. After the honeymoon period, the friction starts and it is common for the new shareholders to need to find an exit route for the founders, whilst replacing their key skills. The problem is so common that there are executive recruitment companies which provide 'founder syndrome' services. This is an extreme, but not unusual, case of the issue that arises when personality traits that are key to one stage of development of an organisation do not fit well with other stages.

Reward for intermediate stages

It has been recognised that the large majority of people have a style that is best suited to a particular stage in the life cycle of an organisation. Organisations can change to a far greater degree than most people can accommodate. The problem is that few individuals recognise this limitation in themselves. When this inevitable progression leads to a change of management, it is frequently conducted in a confrontational manner, which can be damaging to the organisation as well as to the individuals.

Early stage companies are frequently overoptimistic about their chances of success. They typically underestimate the changes that will be required to take the business to a successful and sustainable level. Some early stage investors, including a number of venture capital companies, expect that there will normally be at least two complete changes of management in taking a company from concept to maturity.

The same early stage investors usually try to motivate the first set of directors and managers with stock options which can be heavily diluted by later investment rounds. This dilution frequently leads to a situation where the final board and management get a disproportionately high reward compared to their contribution to the value of the company.

There is a motor racing maxim which states 'if you want to finish first, first you have to finish'. The same logic applies to business. There is a much more fundamental version which states 'if you want to succeed, first you have to survive'. The other analogy that might be used is putting a carrot on the end of a stick to motivate a donkey. Unfortunately for investors, these 'donkeys' can have a much more destructive kick.

Many investors find it much easier to reward a functional distribution, i.e. across a complete management team, than to reward a temporal distribution, i.e. across successive management teams. This situation arises because the financial value of the business typically follows a hockey stick curve, rising on first revenues and then rising much more steeply as profits are generated. This financial value curve does not reflect the distribution of effort and penalises the early stage individuals who are often the creative force.

One option for providing an equitable distribution of rewards is:

- to agree appropriate milestones in the development of the organisation
- to reward the incumbent board and management team appropriately in relation to the real medium to long term financial value of the business
- to use the milestones to review and agree the optimum structure and membership of the board.

This approach allows all concerned to have an open, objective view of the company and their role in it, enabling all parties to move on as required. The limited number of venture capital companies which adopt this solution then re-use the early stage board for new opportunities, thus ensuring that all parties are fully committed.

Those founders who do succeed may well become serial entrepreneurs, generating great wealth for both themselves and for the investors who treat them fairly when they found a company which they can take all the way through to maturity. It ought, therefore, to be in the investors' interest to ensure that they are well compensated to make it more likely that they come back to the same investors with their next opportunity.

Building a board

It is common for boards to be built from scratch, such as in a start-up organisation, or to be re-built when a major new investor comes in, for example when a venture capitalist takes a controlling interest in a company. The functional and risk mapping processes discussed earlier are important tools that can be used here. The four core roles of board dynamics in the Frame Model provide a powerful basis for a board that can be supported by psychometric tests where required. This set of tools greatly assists the initial requirements definition and the selection process. However, there are some significant structural issues that need to be decided. The main issues are getting the size of the board right, getting the chairman's role right, deciding which executives should be on the board and selecting the right non-executives. Once these are established then the emphasis can switch to effective board operation.

Size of the board

An important question is: how big should the board be in order to maximise its effectiveness? There are two answers to this question, depending on what the primary function of the board is. Cost is a significant factor but this must not be a barrier to board effectiveness because the cost of making the wrong decision can be much higher than the cost of an extra board member.

If the board's primary role is to drive the organisation forward and to challenge the executives, as is necessary in early stage and rapidly changing businesses, then its size needs to facilitate the interchange of ideas. As a comparison, a good rule of thumb that is used for brainstorming sessions is to have a group of six people. This is big enough to get a good pool of ideas and to stop one person dominating the group and is small enough not to subdue the quieter members of the group. It is reasonable to assume that a similar logic applies to the boards of many organisations.

It is common in large companies or in public sector organisations for the management team to provide the monitor function for the organisation. In this case the board's primary role is supervisory. The board size can then be much larger, enabling the board to monitor all key aspects of the organisation's performance.

Very small boards can be risky except in small companies with low investment levels and, therefore, correspondingly low risk levels. Many small companies see a board as something that can limit their flexibility. Research has shown that such companies, especially those that do not have independent directors, frequently have little or no strategic vision. Instead they rely on opportunistic development and hope that nothing more complex comes into play.

The role of the chairman

Choosing a chairman is a key decision when building a board. Chairmen must have the right mix of independence, strength, decision-making ability, facilitation skills and interpersonal skills if they are to be able to make the board work effectively.

The role of the chairman is critical to the operation of the board. It is his or her job to ensure that the board makes timely decisions that the majority of the board, and preferably all of it, is committed to. The chairman must be a clear and logical decision maker who can ensure that the board reaches a decision. He or she must have the ability to facilitate open discussion, to draw out the views of the other board members and to arbitrate disagreements between board members. It is very helpful if the chairman can also act as an intermediary to assist in presenting the decisions to stakeholders, including investors and employees where necessary.

In addition to the primary skills required by an effective chairman, there are very important supporting skills that enable the understanding and optimisation of board dynamics, thereby maximising the effectiveness of the board. People who are good man managers generally have an instinctive sense of how to get the best out of both individuals and teams. They constantly assess personalities and match these to the required roles. Good chairmen do the same with board members but they have the extra dimension of board dynamics to play with, provided they have the insight to be able to appreciate and understand this.

Since board members normally only interact with the rest of the board for a small proportion of the time, it is relatively easy for them to adopt a specific facet of their personality, at the instigation of the chairman, to improve the board dynamics. For the board member to agree to this, he or she must have an open, trusting relationship with the chairman which puts further emphasis on the interpersonal skills of the chairman. The chairman ought to have the mentoring skills to establishing such a relationship. This principle does not necessarily apply in family firms where the board members may sometimes have too close a relationship to make objective decisions.

Appraisals provide a powerful tool to enable board members to develop their relationship with the chairman. In the ego-laden environment of the boardroom, this can be a challenge but it is important to achieve objectivity (Example 23).

Example 23

The CEO of a publicly quoted company was insistent that appraisals were carried out throughout the company as he saw this as necessary to ensure effectiveness. However, he drew the line when it came to appraising board members. He took the view that board members were either doing a good job or they would be fired. The inconsistency reflected a difference in styles between the CEO and the chairman. The CEO did not want to be appraised by the chairman and the difference eventually led to a showdown.

Because of the unique challenges of being on a board, it is important that board members are given appraisals specifically focused on their board positions. These should be undertaken by the chairman with assistance from the senior non-executive director. Board appraisals must be distinct from the appraisals conducted for executive directors in their executive roles. If board members do not wish to be appraised then the chairman must seriously question their attitude to their board role. The CEO in this example failed to recognise the importance of the distinction between his operational role and his directorship. His position was dubious in either case as there is always room for constructive comments and criticism even at the highest levels in an organisation.

It is essential that the chairman commands respect and that others trust his or her judgement. It is highly desirable that he or she has insight into the personalities of the other board members. It is also desirable that the other board members trust the chairman as an individual. If all of these criteria are met then the board has a good chance of working effectively as a team provided that there is a reasonable choice of candidates available to it.

It may sound challenging for an individual to take part in an active board discussion whilst undertaking an objective analysis of both the behaviour of individuals and the group dynamics. However, this is something that good man managers do intuitively on a day to day basis. The chairman must take the lead and needs to have good interpersonal skills. Because the chairman might have a problem with certain board members and not fully realise it, he or she must also invite comments from other board members to be made aware of such issues.

Which executives ought to be on the board?

The board must have access to accurate information on, and insight into, the operation of the organisation in order to ensure that the strategy implementation and risks are managed properly. Executives are required to provide this information to board members, not just through the board papers but also by being available for discussion at board meetings. They do not need to be board members or even observers to do the latter. If their opinion is used to steer board decisions rather than just provide information then they should be formal members of the board - having the title of 'director' does not make someone a director in legal terms

Whilst the CEO needs to have a thorough understanding of the whole of the company, specialists are required for key areas. In most organisations, the primary risks are financial and commercial. These require the detailed knowledge of the Finance Director and the Sales & Marketing Director respectively. Technology based companies require a Technical Director to manage the product and technology risks. The choice of executives on the board needs to reflect the key risk areas for that organisation. The detailed structure of the risks often depends on contractual terms such as penalty clauses. Having a lawyer on the board, typically as the company secretary, can help reduce these risks significantly.

It is normal practice in the UK for the CEO to be on the board because, in order to manage the organisation, he or she requires at least the same information as the board and ought, therefore, to be a member of it. Where the lead executive is not on the board, typically being called a general manager, it is likely that he or she is a shadow director of the organisation. This is an unsatisfactory situation which occurs most frequently in family-owned companies.

Because of the importance of the financial results and the technical complexity of accounting, it is normal practice for the Finance Director to be on the board. There need to be compelling reasons for any other executives to be on the board. Board membership should not be granted as a reward or mark of status as there are alternative means of providing this without compromising the operation and effectiveness of the board.

Choosing non-executives

Getting the right balance between the skills and styles of executive and non-executive directors is essential to the success of a board. The chairman, who is usually a non-executive, is a very important appointment. Executive directors are normally appointed because it goes with their management responsibilities so there is far less option to select them on the basis of their personal style.

Choosing NEDs is important both internally, for the operation of the organisation, and externally because of the way it is seen by stakeholders and the outside world. NEDs also provide the greatest scope for getting the right balance of personalities and approaches on a board.

As the responsibilities of board members increase, it is more difficult to find people with the right skills and motivation to take on non-executive positions. The result is that the pool of experienced non-executives has shrunk. This increases the risk that non-executives will be kept on for too many terms of office. The main new source of non-executives is from executive directors of other companies who see non-executive roles as a means of sharpening their skills. Such directors frequently come from larger companies, which may wish their senior executives to broaden their experience by spending time on outside activities, thereby driving a trend in the UK towards 'big company' non-executives.

It is good practice to have a nominations committee, either formal or informal, to manage the process of finding new non-executives. The process of identifying good candidates should be ongoing so that they can be called in when required, even if the change is unplanned. All members of the board ought to have the right to interview candidates prior to appointment and to feed back their opinions to the nominations committee for consideration. All good candidates would want this anyway as part of their induction process.

As discussed above, non-executives should be chosen not only for their experience and functional skills but also for personal styles that will complement the board. The core objective is to find people who add value, who can argue their case clearly and forcefully against strong opposition but who are open and objective enough to work with the decision of the majority. Their personalities should complement the rest of the board and provide a stimulus for constructive and challenging discussions.

Running a board

For a board to be effective, it requires the directors to combine their strengths and experience to make a group decision in the best interests of the organisation. Because of the nature of the board, it is easier to find people with the right skills and experience than it is to make them work together effectively. The latter requires a strong, insightful chairman coupled with careful selection of board members.

Board dynamics make the board work effectively as a group. They can make the whole much greater than the sum of the parts or, conversely, they can make it much less. The key is to find a complementary set of personalities and roles that ensures a challenging but constructive approach to fulfilling the board's role. The differences in personalities can be harnessed as a means of stimulating discussion. Openness and objectivity are key attributes.

Given that the core roles of the board are to make decisions and to identify risks, it is essential that at least the chairman is decisive. If too many board members are very decisive then it can stifle discussion. A facilitative approach is critical to allow board members scope to probe potential risk areas in an open manner.

The chairman and the senior members of the board should make time, separate from board meetings, to discuss how the board is working, the impact of board dynamics on its effectiveness and to address dynamics issues as soon as possible. This is particularly important when new directors join the board to ensure that they are able to play the role that the board expects of them.

By recognising the importance of the human side of the board and managing it effectively, the board stands the best chance of enabling the organisation to deliver excellent and consistent performance. Making use of all reasonable methods, including board dynamics, to manage the organisation also reduces the risk of directors being held liable for any mistakes they might make.

Succession planning

The only thing that is constant is change. All environments are competitive, dynamic and usually both, so organisations need to plan for and accommodate change. The board must be equipped to address and exploit the new opportunities and challenges that arise. It must have a built-in mechanism to change the way it considers options and makes decisions and be able to adapt its structure accordingly. Change should be embraced as a positive opportunity for regeneration. Too often at board level, losing a board position is seen as the loss of a comfortable stipend. Leaving a board ought not to be seen as a failure but simply as the end of a term of office and a time for all parties to move on.

One way to assist the regeneration process is to retrain the board on a regular basis but this can be difficult in practice. However, updating the skills of board members does not necessarily change the way they think and an easier option may be to plan for succession. Changes can be straightforward to make for non-executives who have terms of office, typically for three years, and are subject to re-election. It is more awkward to apply this principle to executive directors as the timing for their executive role may not match their term of office as a director.

The Higgs report (4) recommends that, for public companies, no non-executive should be appointed for a third term of office without very good reason, which is a very sensible approach for all companies. It is not necessarily a bad thing for the non-executives because they will have broader experience to take to their next role and, therefore, may be able to add more to that board.

All directors of UK public companies have to stand for regular re-election. It is rare for an executive director not to be re-elected as this would indicate a massive loss of confidence by the shareholders that the board had not acted upon.

Higgs also emphasises, quite correctly, that it is bad practice for an executive, especially the outgoing CEO, to be appointed as a non-executive in the same company. It is difficult for people to let go the reins of power and such a change may compromise the position of the incoming CEO. It is much less of a problem for a non-executive to be appointed as an executive director, which can sometimes provide a very good solution for an organisation.

A much larger problem arises with private family-owned companies where the non-executives are usually major shareholders or their representatives. Such directors may see their seats on the board as a right rather than a duty. Furthermore, in this scenario one individual can be a non-executive throughout massive changes in the company without anyone querying his or her contribution (Example 24).

Example 24

A technology start-up spent years developing its concept, brought in venture capital funding, re-started with a different technology and eventually went through an IPO. During this process, which lasted nine years, there were at least five general managers and chief executives.

The original investor was a non-executive for the entire period despite the huge changes in structure. The VC firm appointed a partner as a non-executive when it invested and one of its representatives remained on the board for the duration. The only change to the non-executives was to bring in a chairman with the right profile to support the company's flotation.

The question is why executives were changed so frequently when so little change was required amongst the non-executive directors? The answer may be that the investor organisations did not adequately separate their roles as shareholders from their roles of directors. Serious questions must also be raised concerning conflict of interest as these parties might have put their interests as investors ahead of the duties of their representatives as directors.

A sensible term of office without automatic re-election provides a framework to overcome the problem. Unfortunately, many smaller investor organisations do not have the depth of resources to enable a choice of candidate directors with the right skills and experience to allow them to rotate directorships.

Boards with such strong shareholder representation often act as investor management committees rather than true boards. These boards also tend to be small, with independent directors seen as expensive luxuries rather than people who could make a significant contribution to the board. This view makes it even harder to get the board dynamics right and such a structure is a recipe for conflict.

Selection criteria

As discussed earlier, the key dimensions are functionality, risk, experience, communication and dynamics. The first three provide the board with the skills it needs. The last two enable it to perform effectively. An important task for the chairman and the board is to develop a clear view of how the board itself needs to evolve in the medium term. This view underpins any succession planning and it enables the directors to define how the role and personal style of any replacement board member need to differ from those of an incumbent.

The evolving needs of the board are the key drivers of succession planning. The changes in functionality and the shifts in emphasis during the evolution of the organisation should be reflected in the make-up of the board. Classic examples are seen in support functions such as human resources and information technology. Directors with responsibility for these functions occur rarely in young companies but they become more common as the company grows. In due course, the company may grow to a size where they become critical to its operation. However, in very large companies, people in these roles only remain on the board if they are critical to the company's strategic direction rather than being a support function.

Not only can the spread of functions change, the emphasis within a particular function can also change significantly as the company grows. For example, the technical director (TD) in a technology company in a start-up is typically a specialist in the underlying concept behind the business, whereas the TD in a mature company is usually a strategic generalist in technology terms.

The functional map of the organisation (see Chapter 8) can be used to assign priorities to each function. The priorities then define which functional skills require representation on the board and the depth of skill needed. The risk map of the organisation looks at the other critical element; the greater the risk in a particular area, the greater the experience the board requires to manage that area. Both maps should be reviewed before any significant changes are made to the board.

The spread of experience on the board needs to reflect not only the current risks and challenges but also those anticipated within the timescales for which the board expects to make decisions. A broad range of experience is necessary to provide contingency for risk management and have some cover for the unexpected. In selecting new members, what matters is not the length of experience per se but how much the individual has learned from it. These two do not necessarily go hand in hand; it is better to have ten years' experience than one year's experience twenty times over.

Because board dynamics enable the board to function as a team, the selection criteria for new members should take these into account. The core requirements for a balanced board are discussed in chapter 8 and the goal should be to maintain the balance in the medium term. Such an approach to succession planning does not mean it is necessary to find a like for like replacement in terms of personality between the outgoing and incoming directors because the overall dynamics of the board may need to change to reflect the development of the organisation.

Timing

Timing for the replacement of executives and non-executives are very distinct issues. In both cases a planned replacement that is fully understood and agreed by all parties is much better for all concerned. All departures, both planned and unplanned should be treated very fairly as befits the most senior members of the organisation.

The replacement of non-executives can be timed to coincide with their re-election period and to allow a thorough search for the best candidates to replace them. Executive replacement ought to be linked to key milestones that reflect an appropriate limit which makes the best use of the executive's skills. Such milestones should focus on the medium to long term to allow the executives to be fully committed to their tasks. The targets must be agreed openly so that the executives are not looking over their shoulders the whole time. In return, the executives should be rewarded for reaching the milestones. In this respect, the executives may consider their positions more as long-term contractors rather than as normal employees, but they need to be contractors to whom the organisation is fully committed. The reality is that the average tenure of the majority of CEOs and MDs is probably less than that of NEDs.

Unplanned replacements at board level are frequently an indicator of an underlying problem and should be avoided as far as is practical because of the message this sends to investors. A departure may be related to the individual's performance but it is more common for it to be due to either different views about the future direction of the organisation or problems with board dynamics, the two often being inter-related.

If non-executives leave other than at the end of their term, the board is normally able to continue functioning to a sensible standard while replacements are sought. If executives leave in an unplanned manner then it is important to ensure that their roles are covered at board level, either working through the other executive directors, with input from non-board level staff, or bringing in people to report to the board in those functions as required. The rapid replacement of outgoing executives is highly desirable otherwise risk levels can rise significantly.

Issue recognition and diagnosis

Spotting an issue in the board

Where problems do occur they can be painful and difficult for the individuals concerned so they need to be handled sensitively. It is in everyone's interest, both on a personal basis and for the benefit of the organisation, to recognise problems as early as possible and to resolve them quickly. Creating an operating environment that enables issues to be discussed openly not only aids the identification and diagnosis of problems but also probably helps prevent them. An open interaction is unusual and it often comes down to one or two key directors to monitor the situation.

Because the stakes are high for the organisation and the level of personal responsibility is high for the board members, board meetings can easily become more fraught than they need to be. This pressure can bring out less the pleasant characteristics of the board members which in turn may impair the operation of the board and reduce its effectiveness.

Issues are inevitable at board level. If they don't appear it could be because the board is not trying hard enough, which in itself can put the organisation at risk. There are a number of instinctive reactions to issues and these may impact on how the board works. Some are good. Some can be more dangerous than the issue itself. Under pressure, there is a fine line between a constructive challenge and a problem and it is essential to be able to differentiate between. Repeated occurrences make it much easier to recognise an issue but this does nothing to limit the damage that may occur.

The Frame Model provides a basis for assessing how board dynamics issues impact on a board's effectiveness. It offers a way of determining when the challenging interaction between strong characters becomes a problem that requires action to resolve. A problem can be defined as behaviour that prevents the board from operating with strength in one or more of the four core roles of the Frame Model.

The best early indicator of problems with the behaviour of board members is when it seems that some directors are not listening to the arguments that are being put forward because they have already made their mind up on the issue that is being discussed, they are going to allow someone else to make their mind up for them or they are not interested. By the time problems manifest themselves as visible conflict the situation can be quite serious and requires immediate action. Such conflict implies that the mutual respect that underpins effective board operation may be breaking down.

A certain level of assertiveness is an essential part of challenging discussions. The difficulty is in deciding where it crosses the line into behaviour that hinders the expression of reasonable and relevant opinions. This decision relies on the experience and judgment of the chairman coupled with an appreciation of the normal personalities of the board members. There may be more of an underlying problem when a quiet director becomes mildly aggravated than when an argumentative one becomes more forceful than usual.

The problems that can be the most difficult to identify are those where the whole board is drawn in because there is no-one to take an objective view of the issue. Such problems include 'group think' and 'organisational bystanders' (see Chapter 8). They are prime reasons for changing board personnel in order to bring in new ideas and to break commonly held but potentially outdated opinions.

It is important that someone on the board, preferably the chairman, recognises that there is a problem and raises it for discussion, either formally or informally. If the chairman has ensured that the other board members are aware of the principles of board dynamics and that he or she will react quickly to resolve such issues, they can be flagged openly during a board meeting. This is relatively easy where there is a conflict of interest between a director's roles. It is much harder where the problem relates directly to a board member's personality. For personality issues, it is usually better to raise them informally and is certainly better than not to react to them at all. Identifying an issue early makes it much easier to resolve.

Risks within the board

Whilst the board has a primary responsibility to manage risk, it must be recognised that the board itself can be a source of risk to the organisation.

The key issue from the executives executives' viewpoint is 'who is in control of the organisation?' A key issue from the non-executives' viewpoint is 'can the executives demonstrate that they are really in control?' Unfortunately, a common way to exert control at board level is to restrict the flow of information on the basis that 'knowledge is power'. Restricting information and dialogue limits the ability of the board to see through issues and identify potential problems. Therefore, any battle for control is likely to increase risk levels significantly.

Executive directors are not the only source of risk. For example, there is a potential conflict of interest for non-executive directors who directly represent shareholders because balancing the company's risk and balancing the investors' risk might require very different things.

One of the biggest sources of risk is where the board assumes that its decisions have been implemented or it believes the organisation's own hype. Statements such as 'safety is our biggest concern' are usually generated to set a priority, become true when the priority has been set but can easily be taken for granted and slip back to become a mantra rather than a reality.

Identifying and managing risks are critical parts of the board's role. It is an area where directors, in particular the executives, can feel threatened because some types of risk imply that they are not doing their job thoroughly. An open interchange of information and views is essential. Getting the right board dynamics is crucial if this aspect of board operation is to be effective.

Understanding and differentiating the roles of each board member are important but difficult steps towards achieving this. Most directors have other roles and, as directors, they ought to be capable of challenging themselves in the other roles. When executive directors have additional roles, for example as shareholders or family members, then the situation is even more complex. The key is for the individuals to recognise that there is a potential conflict between the various roles and that this conflict can increase the risk to the organisation as a whole.

Issue diagnosis & resolution

In addition to enabling the identification of board dynamics problems, the Frame Model suggests what needs to be done to resolve them. The list of personality types in Chapter 6 can be used as a guide to help assess the problematic behaviour and thereby understand what action needs to be taken to resolve it.

The core requirements for diagnosing issues on the board are awareness and understanding of the principles and issues that underlie them. A 'Catch 22' arises because boards which have these skills are less likely to have problems and those that do not may not recognise they need them until it is either too late or a perceptive outsider, such as a major shareholder, persuades them otherwise.

In most cases, once a problem has been recognised then it is clear what action needs to be taken to modify the behaviour of the individuals concerned. Simple issues can be resolved by good chairmanship of the board meetings to ensure that each board member contributes to the discussion in an appropriate manner. At this stage it is unlikely that the problems will have a significant detrimental impact on the board's effectiveness and a quiet word from the chairman can help to achieve an early resolution.

When a more complex problem has been identified, the initial step is for the chairman to talk in private to the potentially offending individuals. He or she should remind them of their joint and several responsibility for the board's decisions and try to understand why they behaved in that way. This helps the chairman to get to the heart of the problem but such discussions need to be thought through very carefully. If the chairman is the problem then the senior non-executive must take the lead in resolving the issue.

Since board dynamics problems arise because of directors' personalities, it is often difficult for them to recognise and accept that the problem lies with them. It is far more likely that they will see the problem as being caused by other members of the board. The more reasonable and open-minded the individuals are, the easier it is for the chairman to ask the directors to modify their behaviour. However, people of this type are far less likely to cause problems in the first place.

The resolution of problems with more difficult board members is effectively a process of mediation where the chairman guides the offenders towards a more reasonable position or asks them to take on a slightly different role within the board in order to reduce the risk of damaging conflict. If this process does not work then it is possible to use coaching or training to help the board members concerned. Normally it is only worth considering this option if the individual with the problem brings something special to the board, otherwise it is easier to remove or replace the person concerned. Before getting rid of a board member, the chairman should discuss the proposed action with the other senior directors and the main shareholders to ensure that they understand why the step is necessary and to obtain their support.

For non-executive directors, replacement is normally the preferred option in order to maintain the balance on the board. If those non-executives represent significant stakeholders then it might be difficult to replace them for political reasons. In that case the chairman needs, where possible, to talk to the stakeholders directly, for example to the CEO of a venture capital investor, to see if alternatives are available. For smaller companies, even this may not be an option because the directors may themselves be the shareholders. In the latter case, it can be very difficult for the board to operate effectively and the chairman and other directors should consider their personal positions very carefully and assess the risks and liabilities that they face.

If the issue is with an executive director then it may make more sense in the short term to simply remove him or her from the board but keep them as an executive. However, if this does happen then it is likely that the executive would see that as a block on his or her career and so would seek employment elsewhere.

A critical element in diagnosing an issue is to determine whether a problematic interaction between board members is caused by one of the individuals or more than one. If the problem is based on the interaction between two individuals then the chairman must deal with them separately and act as a mediator. If there are two or more problem directors then the board has a serious issue, especially if it is small, and the risks to the other board members may be increased to an unreasonable level. Severe action needs to be taken in this case, probably involving the removal of all offending board members.

Board checklists

Purpose of the checklists

The discussions in this book have raised a lot of issues concerning boards and the way in which they operate. These have been summarised in the form of checklists as an aide memoire to assist chairs and board members build and maintain an effective board.

Recruitment and renewal

Is the role of the board and its interaction with the executive team and key stakeholders fully defined and understood?

- Is there a clear understanding of the balance of the board that is required in the short and medium term in relation to skills, stakeholder representation, personal styles, gender and/or culture?
- Is this understanding reviewed on a regular basis and the shape of the board adjusted accordingly?
- Is the size of the board appropriate to the needs of the organisation?
- Are there sufficient independent board members to ensure unbiased decision making?
- Does someone have specific responsibility for recruiting new board members and replacing existing ones?
- Is the recruitment process thorough and would it stand up to external assessment if so requested by the shareholders?
- Are any psychometric tests used to assess candidates' personalities? If so, do these tests indicate a possible clash with the existing board members?

- Are references used to get an understanding of the candidate's behaviour on boards as well as to verify their skill level and experience?
- Is the recruitment process open to a wide enough pool of talent?
- Is there a formal induction process for new board members?
- Are new board members fully aware of their legal, personal and operational responsibilities?
- Are new board members made aware of the roles of their colleagues and given the opportunity to understand the personal styles of their colleagues?
- Is the term of office of directors defined and is there an agreed policy for re-election?
- Do the terms of engagement of board members have an appropriate termination clause in addition to their term of office?
- Are the chairman and senior non-executive director strong enough and do they have sufficient backing from the main stakeholders to change board members when necessary?

Operating and decision making

- Does the chairman have a good working knowledge of corporate governance?
- Is the chairman independent?
- Are potential conflicts of interest between their various roles fully understood by the board members concerned and the chairman?
- Is the board well balanced in terms of the four roles of the Frame Model?
- Do the board members have the right background and personal skills for their role in this level of organisation?

- Are all members willing and able to give and accept constructive challenges?
- Is there a regular appraisal process in place?
- Does each board member ensure that they are adequately prepared for board meetings and discussions?
- Is the level of communication between board members adequate both in board meetings and outside?
- Are issues discussed openly and to sufficient depth in board meetings?
- Are board discussions thorough, challenging and conducted in a constructive manner?
- Are board discussions kept to the point?
- Do all members make a full contribution to board meetings?
- Is the information provided to the board at the right level and available in a timely manner?
- Do board members have adequate access to the executive team for discussions?
- Does the board make use of external advisers to assist their decision making process where appropriate?
- Are board members given enough time and information to make balanced, reasonable and justifiable decisions?
- Is the board sufficiently aware of market trends and external factors to identify opportunities?
- Are risks being identified and addressed correctly and would the monitoring processes stand up to external scrutiny?
- Does the board enable the executive team to operate effectively whilst providing adequate monitoring and support?

- Are discussions and decisions clearly and concisely minuted to demonstrate that the board is operating effectively?
- Are specific board roles, such as senior non-executive director, fully defined and understood?
- Is the board committee structure clear and are the roles of the committees fully defined?
- Is the interaction between the chairman and the CEO effective?
- Is the level of interaction and reporting between nominated board members and the main shareholders sufficiently frequent and at an appropriate level?
- Are formal reporting requirements met and standard codes of practice adhered to?
- Have specific board members been given responsibility for corporate communications and have they been trained for this role?

Problem analysis and rectification

- Do the chairman and senior non-executive director have a good knowledge of board dynamics issues and their ramifications?
- Where appropriate, have board members been made aware of the principles of board dynamics and do they understand what action will be taken to rectify problems?
- Does the chairman have a reasonable appreciation of the personalities and the strengths and weaknesses of each of the board members?
- Does the chairman have the required interpersonal skills to deal with board dynamics issues?
- Are any board members risking a conflict of interest with any of their other roles?

- Do any board members exhibit some characteristics of challenging personality traits?
- Does the board have sufficient information to make a decision?
- Do board meetings have open discussions with contributions from all board members?
- Are board discussions open and are any board members being dominant or too quiet?
- Are problem areas associated with particular topics, individuals or pairs of individuals?

In ascending order of severity, the options for rectification are:

- steering the board discussion
- the chairman telling an individual or individuals to modify their approach
- a private discussion between the chairman and the offending board member(s)
- training or coaching the board member(s) where appropriate
- replacement of the board member(s)

Summary

The objective of this book is to provide an insight into how boards work and the ways in which board members can constrain or impair their operation. It is targeted at chairmen, senior board members and others who are responsible for board monitoring, recruitment and operation and provides an insight for current and aspiring board members. It describes how different types of board work and how board dynamics – the personal interaction between board members – can have a critical impact on board effectiveness.

The role of a board is to protect and guide an organisation on behalf of its stakeholders. The board takes the role of a guardian. It has to allow the organisation scope to operate and develop whilst minimising the risk and maximising its chances of success. The nature of organisations varies considerably and the structure and style of the board need to match the needs of the organisation.

There are different roles within the board itself, each with different challenges. The chairman has a major input to board operation and effectiveness. Non-executives can provide breadth and experience. Independent non-executives offer impartial input but are sadly lacking in many SMEs. Executive directors have to balance their operational roles with their positions as directors. It is the role of the board to guide and protect the organisation and of the executive team to deliver the agreed strategy. Effective interaction between the board and the executive team is crucial to success. Board members can have a number of roles in addition to being a director or an executive, for example being a shareholder. Multiple roles create the potential for a conflict of interest when a director adopts the wrong role during interactions with the board. It is very important that multiple roles are understood and monitored carefully to protect the board and the organisation.

In order to be successful, the board must be able to make balanced decisions on certain key issues. The main balancing factors are reflected in the core roles of the Frame Model. The four roles form two opposing pairs: the high level view versus the detailed view and opportunistic risk-taking versus risk management. The interaction between these roles creates a tension that is necessary to drive the organisation forward but it is also a potential source of conflict. Managing these conflicts in a constructive manner is essential because a board without constructive conflict will fail.

The four roles of the Frame Model reflect four forces that define the dynamics of the organisation. Therefore, the internal balance of the board is also a primary driver of the overall behaviour of the organisation. The board needs to reflect the nature of the organisation not only in terms of its focus but also its stage of development. As organisations grow and develop, the board must change its personnel and its approach to reflect the changing needs. Even if organisations appear to be stable, they are still subject to the vagaries of a rapidly changing world. Such instability in their operating environment may affect the organisation significantly and thereby necessitate a different approach. The evolution of the board and its membership must be planned carefully. The plan should not only maintain the right interaction within the board but also ensure the right skills and experience are in place to suit both the current and planned phases in the evolution of the organisation.

Board meetings need to be challenging and, when required, confrontational but in a constructive way. The members of the board must ensure that the organisation is moving in the right direction in an appropriate manner and with an acceptable level of risk. Boards require a group of able, strong-willed people to work together effectively as a decision making and monitoring unit. These individuals also bear a high level of personal risk. In order to get onto a board, its members should have demonstrated exceptional capability in some form, usually a combination of expertise, experience and insight. Such people may become used to getting their own way as a result of their success. They are often experienced leaders who must in turn enable the executives to lead rather than lead themselves. Putting a group of able people together on a board provides great strength and a great opportunity. It can also create great weakness if the interaction between these strong individuals becomes detrimental to the board and the organisation.

Board dynamics can have a radical impact on the effectiveness of the board. They need to be understood and managed carefully, preferably by the chairman, to ensure that their effects are minimised. Given the strength of characters in the boardroom, managing meetings can be a major challenge. When potential problems arise they must be tackled as early as possible. An understanding of the principles of board dynamics provides a sound framework for the diagnosis and rectification of problems. It also allows the board to operate in a flexible manner because all of its members appreciate the ground rules that underpin their interactions.

The constraints on the choice of board members, especially for small organisations, make it imperative that board behaviour is managed to maintain effectiveness. If problems do lead to difficulties for the organisation then the board members need to remind themselves of their personal liabilities. If there were solutions available for board dynamics problems and they were not used then the board members risk being seen as negligent.

Having board members who think differently can help board discussions. Diversity on a board, through gender or culture, can be a powerful way of achieving this. However, there may be further complexities when either the membership of the board or the remit of the organisation crosses cultures and nationalities. A multicultural team can increase the likelihood of misunderstanding but the benefits can also be very significant. Board members need to recognise any culture differences that exist on the board and adjust their ways of working to accommodate the diversity. The board also needs to understand how its dictates will be interpreted and implemented by other cultures and should modify these where necessary to achieve the desired outcome.

The chairman is responsible for managing the board. He or she needs to understand not only the organisation but also the personalities of the other board members in order to ensure balanced, reasonable and justifiable decision making. This requires him or her to be able to drive through the ongoing renewal of board members, including his or her own role, and to manage board dynamics issues as they arise. He or she also has a critical relationship with the CEO which will inform, support and monitor the CEO and thereby the whole executive team.

The key components in understanding, managing and developing a board are to:

- Review the role of the board by taking account of the:
  - Nature of the organisation
  - Development stage of the organisation
  - Strength of the management team
  - Interaction between the board and the executive team
- Assess the current position and identify improvements by reviewing the:
  - Functional skills and relevant experience
  - Internal and external politics
  - Roles and personalities
  - Assessment of the four roles of the Frame Model
  - Current status of the organisation and its environment
  - Organisation dynamics
- Clarify vision and values by:
  - Checking for common understanding
  - Openness to new ideas and challenges
  - Maximising the effectiveness of the board as a team
- Correct dysfunctional behaviour by:
  - Identifying problem areas
  - Diagnosing causes
  - Rectifying the behaviour or replacing board members

Note that all of these components are ongoing tasks, the only difference being the frequency with which they have to be revisited.

Major failings at board and corporate level in recent years have lead to an increase in the personal responsibilities and accountabilities of board members. This is fair. Board members must respond with greater thoroughness and dedication based on a sound understanding not only of the organisation but also of the way in which the board itself works.

References

1. Meredith Belbin, "Management Teams", Butterworth-Heinemann, 2004 (latest edition).
2. Geoffrey A Moore, "Crossing the Chasm", Capstone, 1999.
3. Ann Kelly, "Review of "The rise and fall of Marks & Spencer ... and how it rose again" by Judi Bevan", Professional Manager, July 2007, page 42.
4. Derek Higgs, "Review of the role and effectiveness of non-executive directors", Department of Trade and Industry, 2003.
5. "The Combined Code on Corporate Governance", Financial Reporting Council, 2008 (latest edition).
6. "Public Company Accounting Reform and Investor Protection Act of 2002", (Sarbanes-Oxley Act), USA Federal Law, 2002.
7. Williams, Bertsch, Dale, van der Wiele, van Iwaarden, Smith & Visser, "Quality and risk management: what are the key issues?", The TQM Magazine, Vol. 18, no. 1, 2006.
8. Kees van der Heijden, "Scenarios: The Art of Strategic Conversation", Wiley & Sons, 2004 (2nd edition).
9. Turnbull, "Internal control: revised guidance for directors on the combined code", Financial Reporting Council, 2005.
10. Smith, "Guidance on audit committees", Financial Reporting Council, 2008.

11. Laura Tyson, “The Tyson Report on the Recruitment and Development of Non-Executive Directors”, London Business School, 2003.
12. “Building Better Boards”, Department of Trade and Industry, 2004.
13. Abraham H Maslow, “A theory of human motivation”, Psychological Review 50(4), 1943, pp370-96.
14. Hoggett Bowers, “NHS Chief Executives ‘Bold and Old’”, Hoggett Bowers, 2009.
15. Isabel Briggs Myers, “Gifts Differing: Understanding Personality Type”, Davies-Black Publishing, 1980
16. Bioss International, www.biosseurope.com/bioss Framework.htm
17. Allyn Freeman, “The Leadership Genius of Alfred P. Sloan: Invaluable Lessons on Business, Management, and Leadership for Today’s Manager”, McGraw-Hill, 2005.
18. D. A Kolb. & R. Fry, “Toward an applied theory of experiential learning” in C. Cooper (ed.) “Theories of Group Process”, John Wiley, 1975
19. Venturecast Newsletter Issue 58, 15th May 2007, Library House.
20. Fons Trompenaars & Charles Hampden-Turner, “Riding The Waves of Culture: Understanding Diversity in Global Business”, McGraw-Hill, 1997.
21. Geert Hofstede & Gert Jan Hofstede, “Cultures and Organizations: Software of the Mind”, McGraw-Hill, 2005 (2nd edition).
22. Geert Hofstede, “Geert Hofstede Cultural Dimensions web site”, www.geert-hofstede.com.
23. “Japanese culture – a primer”, www.thejapanfaq.com/FAQ-Primer.html.
24. Trompenaars & Woolliams, “When two worlds collide” in “Financial Times Handbook of Management”, FT Publishing, 2001 (2nd edition).

25. Marc Gerstein with Michael Ellsberg, "Flirting with Disaster: Why Accidents Are Rarely Accidental", Sterling, 2008.
26. Boardroom Associates, www.boardroomassociates.co.uk.
27. Eric Berne, "Games People Play – The Basic Hand Book of Transactional Analysis", Ballantine Books, 1964.

Lightning Source UK Ltd.
Milton Keynes UK
UKOW051009170412

190892UK00001B/4/P

9 781907 211126